SACRED SYNERGY

SACRED SYNERGY

Spiritual & Psychological Growth in an Evolving World

Pierre Teilhard de Chardin,
Carl Jung & Roberto Assagioli

ANDREW DEL ROSSI

Paulist Press
New York / Mahwah, NJ

Cover image by maxximmm1 / DepositPhotos
Cover design by Sharyn Banks
Book design by Lynn Else

Library of Congress Cataloging-in-Publication Data
Names: Del Rossi, Andrew author
Title: Sacred synergy: spiritual & psychological growth in an evolving world : Pierre Teilhard de Chardin, Carl Jung, & Roberto Assagioli / Andrew Del Rossi.
Description: Paperback. | New York : Paulist Press, [2026] | Includes bibliographical references. | Summary: "This book is an integrated analysis of Pierre Teilhard de Chardin's evolutionary spirituality in conversation with the psychotherapeutic work of Carl Jung and Roberto Assagioli"—Provided by publisher.
Identifiers: LCCN 2025037559 (print) | LCCN 2025037560 (ebook) | ISBN 9780809157822 paperback | ISBN 9780809189502 ebook
Subjects: LCSH: Teilhard de Chardin, Pierre | Jung, Carl | Assagioli, Roberto, 1888–1974 | Spirituality—Psychology | Psychotherapy—Religious aspects—Catholic Church
Classification: LCC B2430.T374 D375 2026 (print) | LCC B2430.T374 (ebook)
LC record available at https://lccn.loc.gov/2025037559

LC ebook record available at https://lccn.loc.gov/2025037560

ISBN 978-0-8091-5782-2 (paperback)
ISBN 978-0-8091-8950-2 (ebook)

Published by Paulist Press
997 Macarthur Boulevard
Mahwah, NJ 07430
www.paulistpress.com

Printed and bound in the
United States of America

For Mary and our children

Contents

Acknowledgements

I am especially thankful for my teachers and mentors, now turned friends and colleagues, who have inspired and challenged me, and been in my corner as I have worked to develop my ideas and my writing: Kathy Duffy, Tom Legere, Frank Berna, Lou Savary, John Haught, Jim Brady, and Joe Marquart.

I am indebted for the connections and friendships made with members and associates of the American Teilhard Association. It is comforting and motivating to have found a community I can call "my people."

I want to express my deep gratitude for the Norbertine community at Daylesford Abbey. It is a pleasure to serve with you and I am immensely grateful for you welcoming my family and supporting my work.

Finally, I am forever thankful for my wife, Mary, and our family. You are all a perpetual reminder of the flame of love that brings the universe into being.

Introduction

For many years, I have been studying Pierre Teilhard de Chardin's life and thought. I have found in him a way to reconcile a healthy and integrated understanding of both spirituality and psychology. He illuminated pathways for me so that theology and psychology complement each other. He honored the uniqueness of each person even as he valued the journey of humanity itself. His ability to reconcile all these things enabled me to see a fuller picture of our inner world that I want to share. Like Teilhard, my hope is that, together, we can find our way to evolve, individually and collectively, toward God.

I wrote *Sacred Synergy* hoping to provide seekers with a spiritual journey that is both enlightening and empowering. May it help guide you, as it has me, toward a sense of fullness and wholeness during life's complexities.

In this book, I delve into the universal themes of connection, balance, and self-discovery. Two contemporaries of Teilhard—Carl Jung and Roberto Assagioli—will provide insightful reflections with deep psychological and spiritual wisdom. Teilhard focused on consciousness within an evolving world. Jung enriched his thought by exploring and sketching the unconscious part of the psyche. Then, Assagioli showed how to synthesize or integrate the whole psyche. Together, the three thinkers give a much fuller and richer psychological picture of the "playing field" on which to develop a healthy spirituality and a clearer path to spiritual growth in today's world.

As evolution unfolds around us, it also unfolds within us. Our inner world becomes the conscious crucible where we do the necessary work to transform first ourselves, and then the world.

1

Living in an Evolving World

In all chaos there is a cosmos, in all disorder a secret order.

Carl Jung, *The Archetypes and the Collective Unconscious*

If your journey is anything like mine, you may come to find the work of Pierre Teilhard de Chardin, Carl Jung, and Roberto Assagioli to be deeply comforting, challenging, and inspiring. Our current world situation seems as though many, if not all, of our geopolitical, cultural, environmental, ecclesial, and technological spheres are in peril. We can encounter both the hope found in the depths of the minds, as well as the wisdom in the hearts, of these figures as they sought integral wholeness—each in a unique way.

These thinkers all lived during great periods of global unrest covering World Wars I and II, when the very language of a world at war implied that all was in a state of chaos, all was for naught. Teilhard witnessed horrors beyond the comprehension of the collective psyche of his time. Serving as a stretcher bearer in the French Army during World War I, he was immersed in the bloodiness of trench warfare in the European theater. For the first time in the history of warfighting, human eyes watched as the machines of war and the products of the Industrial Revolution—tanks, armored vehicles, artillery, and even chemical weapons—were unleashed on a mass scale as the human organism groaned and wailed in conflict against itself. He also lived through World War II and witnessed the destructive potential of nuclear energy. Despite his service to and love for his home country of France, he was exiled from his beloved homeland because he was pursuing his inspired vision. This was, undoubtedly, a heavy burden for Teilhard to carry, as he was simultaneously forbidden from publishing his inspired theological and spiritual insights.

Psychiatrist Carl Jung, a contemporary of Teilhard, also felt the psychic weight of the First and Second World Wars. Jung was particularly astonished by the almost mystical psychological power of a figure like Adolf Hitler. Jung possessed a sense of the impending doom and destruction that would result from the global conflict, acquired while sifting through the waves of images and feelings that he wrestled with in his own, personal psychological work. Yet even before Jung had tapped into a sense of a conflict in the larger, collective psyche, he was exposed to this kind of tension on the interpersonal level and within himself though his affiliation with his mentor, Sigmund Freud. Their relationship had a falling out and it was cataclysmic for Jung.

While the details of Teilhard's and Jung's personal lives are rather well-known, the personal details of psychiatrist Roberto Assagioli's life are not as public. It is noted that Assagioli was intentional about his privacy. This is understandable when we consider Assagioli's life. He served as a medical doctor in

World War I, an experience of which he never spoke. He was later arrested and kept in a solitary cell by Mussolini's government for twenty-seven days, accused of "praying for peace and inviting others to join him along with other international crimes."[1] His family's farm in Florence would be destroyed in World War II. Assagioli and his family went into hiding, where his son, his only child, would die.

Despite the challenges and apparent dead-ends that these three men faced, they were able to use their experiences as "grist for the mill." They maintained the ability to be immersed within the deep sense of psychological distress of their time and of their own lives without succumbing to the looming doubt, despair, and darkness that surrounded them. By journeying within themselves and through exploring their inner worlds, they were able to get a better perspective through which to engage the outer world.

Although Teilhard's experience in war was traumatic on many levels, the experience opened him spiritually and psychologically with a cosmic perspective of God. The destruction of Jung's personal and professional relationship with Freud, along with some other personal relationships he had with women, were catalysts to send Jung spiraling into his own psychic episode. He lived in seclusion, for a time, where he developed many of his seminal ideas on the psyche. After Europe's liberation and the end of World War II, Assagioli and his family emerged from hiding in the Swiss Alps and returned to their life in Italy. It was then that Assagioli found peace and honed his work on psychosynthesis.

In the face of chaos, these thinkers found a cosmos. They discovered the "secret order," if you will, of the evolutionary spiral that ascends through time and space, winding and reaching for higher states of purpose, relationship, and being. Suffering, challenge, conflict, tension, and so many other "undesirables" are very much part and parcel of the process of evolution. These three men, Teilhard, Jung and Assagioli, discovered that facing and engaging these conflicts consciously is the only way to bring them into the light.

The chapters that follow are an exploration of Teilhard's life and thought in a way that seeks to reconcile a healthy and integrated understanding of both spirituality and psychology. He illuminates pathways where theology and psychology can complement each other. He honors the uniqueness of each person even as he valued the journey of humanity itself. His ability to reconcile all these things enabled him to paint for us a fuller picture of our inner world, so that we can find our way to evolve, individually and collectively, toward God.

The lesson he taught us is that, if we don't do this inner work, we can quickly become overwhelmed by the unconscious mind presenting itself as shadowy figures, states, suspicions, and circumstances conspiring against us. Even worse, we fail to recognize that this outer reality is, in part, a reflection of the turmoil and lack of peace in the world within ourselves. This dynamic has resulted in an egoic individualism that has created the illusion of separateness within the world.

Meanwhile, the leading fields of research, from hard sciences such as biology and physics to soft sciences such as psychology and anthropology, are discovering how deeply and intimately interconnected the world is. We depend upon one another. Furthermore, this interrelatedness on a material level is also indicating that there is an increase in consciousness—a more integrated awareness of the whole. As things increase in complexity, they have the capacity to become more conscious.

As human persons we possess the gift of having the natural biological capacity, as well as the tools at its disposal, to assist evolution's ascent toward this integration. Against that affirmation, it appears as if our collective trajectory is moving otherwise. Words such as *chaotic, corrupt, disordered, unjust,* and *hateful* tend to dominate our descriptions of the world and our interpersonal dynamics.

I would like to challenge this sentiment through the idea that, by a greater collective recognition of this troubling sense within the world, there is simultaneously a rise in awareness of connection and relationship within it. The true test going forward depends on how we act. More importantly, the future rests on how we orient our being upon this knowing and how we do the work to live more integrated lives. In *Psychology and Alchemy*, Jung writes,

> No matter how much parents and grandparents may have sinned against the child, the man who is really an adult will accept these sins as his own condition which has to be reckoned with. Only a fool is interested in other people's guilt, since he cannot alter it. The wise man learns only from his own guilt. He will ask himself: "Who am I that all this should happen to me?" To find the answer to this fateful question he will look into his own heart.[2]

While we are entwined within complex networks of systems, we are not necessarily consciously integrated into these relationships. The year 2020 marked an inflection point of consciousness when, through a global pandemic, there emerged a collective recognition of how interconnected and interdependent the human species, human systems, and the systems of the natural world are with one another. Separateness, no matter how hard it was politicked, preached, or policed, proved to be unsustainable.

Calling this an "inflection point" does not mean that the illusion of separateness was dispelled and the light of knowing was revealed. Isolation and injustice are still very serious issues on a global scale. This turning point implies simply that humanity is more aware of its interconnectedness than ever before. With access to technology and the internet at an all-time high, humanity is connected, at least in a technological way, now more than ever.

Our challenge going forward is to connect with ourselves and with the world on a more integral level through looking into our hearts. Teilhard affirms, "It is not a tête-à-tête or a corps-à-corps that we need; it is a heart-to-heart."[3] It will not be action toward a common cause or a common way of thinking that will bring humanity and the world together. It will be a common *being* emanating from our hearts and from the heart of the world in which we are united.

SEEKING WHOLENESS THROUGH AN INTERDISCIPLINARY LENS

Looking toward the future, individualism will be challenged by the new paradigm of a world defined by increasing interconnectivity and interdependence. The globalization of society calls for us to grow in our awareness of ourselves and our place within the larger network of being. Thus, we face the challenge of adapting our worldview by embracing a more integrated perspective. We recognize that we do not find fulfillment and a sense of wholeness in isolation, but through relationship. For centuries, humanity has sought wholeness through religions, spiritual practices, and wisdom traditions. Even though postmodernity has begun to turn humanity away from institutionalized spiritual practice, it is critical for seekers to discover the rich treasures found in these traditions that are wellsprings for ways of living a life of fullness and wholeness.

The word *religion* is derived from the Latin *re-ligare*, meaning to re-bind or re-connect, and should dispel the illusion of separateness between humanity and God. *Spirituality* is an expression of the unique ways that we connect to the Divine. Spirituality is what makes religion work at its core. However, healthy spirituality is not always cultivated or encouraged by institutionalized religion. Yet, the variety of ways to connect that are found in the world's religious, spiritual, and wisdom traditions are a beautiful testament to the many ways we can unite and discover wholeness.

Spirituality and psychology lead the human person to wholeness by connecting us to ourselves, others, and the world. Healthy spirituality provides a pathway for us to connect in a personal way with God. The goal of psychology is to study and practice therapeutic methods of directing one to a life of health, happiness, and wholeness. Both spirituality and psychology are roadmaps to greater and fuller being through an understanding of oneself, the world, and the great mystery of being that is beyond logical comprehension.

Teilhard's spirituality, thought, and mysticism are an invaluable guide for an evolving world. He understands the universe as evolving toward a point of wholeness and maximum connectivity, the Omega Point. The human person is a phenomenon within evolution, according to Teilhard, because the human possesses the unique capacity for advanced self-awareness. We are the universe having become self-aware, able to reflect on its existence and contemplate its purpose. Teilhard eventually grew to see how the Divine Presence permeates all of creation. As a result, he became aware of the Divine within his own being.

Teilhard encountered God in such a real and personal way that he was transformed, and he committed his life to what he describes as the "road of fire."[4] The road of fire is the route that leads the universe toward greater wholeness. Each time we recognize the Divine within ourselves and take up the road of fire, humanity draws closer to uniting as an organism, and evolution becomes a greater expression of the Divine within the world.

Teilhard was influenced by his study of the Eastern Church (Greek) fathers, who recognized a dynamic study of the universe's origin. The Greek fathers wrote about *divinization*, or how we are made whole in union with God. Teilhard noted that as we grow more conscious, we develop a higher sense of authenticity of being and purpose, connecting us to the world in more personal and more meaningful ways. Thus, the thinking of the Eastern fathers resonated with Teilhard as he saw humanity growing more aware and uniting in a consciousness of love and relationship. His mystical writings provide insight into his spiritual evolution and his psychological growth toward personal wholeness. When Christ teaches that "you must be perfect just as your heavenly Father is perfect" the word *perfect* is derived from the Greek *teleios*, originating from *telos*. "The word does not mean 'perfect' without blemish but perfected as brought to one's completion or end state."[5] Teilhard challenges us to experience and embody holiness as *wholiness*.

Teilhard's faith provided him with stability in his quest for God. It allowed him to pursue his vision, despite the many challenges he faced throughout his lifetime. His spiritual life gave his psyche the support it needed so that he could express himself and his ideas as authentically as possible. Likewise, psychology also seeks authenticity. It empowers us to grow in awareness of the many parts and dynamics of our inner lives.

The integration of spirituality and psychology illuminates a more thorough understanding of human wholeness in the complexity of the twenty-first century by cultivating a consciousness of interbeing, interconnectedness, and interdependence.

When we explore these two fields in relation to one another, we discover how their interaction provides deeper insight into the *whole*. We discover a sacred synergy.

"IN THE BEGINNING THERE WERE NOT COLDNESS AND DARKNESS: THERE WAS THE FIRE"[6]

Pierre Teilhard de Chardin was born on May 1, 1881, in his family's château of Sarcenat, near the provincial capital, Clermont-Ferrand, France. His father was an amateur naturalist, and his mother was devoted to her Catholic faith. Thus, influenced by a love of the world and a love of God, Teilhard would eventually become a priest in the Society of Jesus while also earning his doctorate in paleontology. Teilhard began a promising academic career teaching chemistry and physics at the Jesuit College of the Holy Family in Cairo, Egypt. After taking time to study theology in the United Kingdom, Teilhard served as a laboratory and field researcher at the National Museum of Natural History in Paris. In 1914, during World War I, Teilhard was mobilized, at the age of thirty-three, as a stretcher bearer in the 8th Moroccan Rifle division of the French Army. After the war, he traveled to China to perform research in the field. He spent the remainder of his life traveling for lectures and conferences and as a researcher for the Wenner-Gren Foundation of Anthropological Research. Teilhard died in New York City on Easter Sunday, April 10, 1955.

Teilhard's scientific reflections and visionary experiences provide insight on the evolution of the universe, the place of the human person, and how human wholeness is achieved through integral relationship with the Divine. His vision is rooted in his empirical observational skills as a scientist along with his understanding of the theological anthropology of the Eastern Church fathers. His theological and spiritual ideas were influential for Karl Rahner, Henri de Lubac, and other theologians whose thought contributed to the developments of the Second Vatican Council.

His influence also extends to the scientific and philosophical communities. Teilhard popularized the concept of the noosphere, or the evolutionary layer of mind and noetic activity, along with Vladamir Vernadsky. He introduced the idea of the Omega Point, or the state of total conscious union in the universe. Teilhard's concept of the Omega Point has been influential on cosmologists, physicists, futurists, architects, and science fiction authors.

Teilhard envisioned a future that was characterized by the universe, and thus the human person, reaching for higher states of being and wholeness. The crux of Teilhard's thought is that evolution is in a process of spiritualization. According to his understanding, evolution is growing into more complex forms of being, resulting in higher levels of consciousness of being, and eventually expressing self-awareness, embodied foremost today in the human person. At the height of one's being, the human person unites with others so that the entire human organism can evolve to possess and exhibit a higher awareness of the spiritual power of matter, of the Divine within our being. This endeavor requires that we "test every barrier, try every path, plumb every abyss"[7] to discern the way forward. Teilhard's faith was dynamic and integral. His faith was not satisfied by the God encountered only in teaching or text, and therefore, in the mind. Teilhard's yearning was for the Divine found everywhere and in *all things*: within matter, within the earth, and within the human person.

In addition to Teilhard's faith was his spirit of hope. Teilhard's hope was driven by his mystic vision where "the future is more beautiful than all the pasts."[8] Ironically enough, his mystical sense was amplified during his military service, where, in witnessing the brutality of war, he also observed humanity's capability to organize and orient itself in union toward a common focus. Teilhard writes that this focus "is finally to be sought, not in the sole contemplation of a single

Truth or in the sole desire for a single Thing, but in the common attraction exercised by a single *Being*."[9]

He saw this movement as a "synthesis of the Spirit" that would be brought about by "the meeting, *center to center*, of human units...realized in a universal, mutual love."[10] These human units, "innumerably diverse by nature, can love one another...by knowing themselves all to be centered upon a single 'supercenter' common to all, to which they can only attain, each at the extreme of himself, through their unity."[11] So, in many ways, the hope that I have observed Teilhardians to exude is not loud and pompous; rather, it is humble and trusts "in the slow work of God,"[12] as Teilhard himself has said.

It is a hope that acknowledges there is much work to be done, and that it will take a long time to get it done; yet, every small task we engage and complete with conscious intention is stitching a thread within the cosmic tapestry. This hope also springs from going inside oneself to do the inner work necessary to grow in consciousness, or self-awareness. This work can also be slow and often feels tedious, taking place over an entire lifetime. Yet, when we do the difficult work necessary to not simply relieve ourselves of these traumas, hang-ups, and ruts in which we get stuck psychologically and spirituality, but we can *integrate* them into our human experience, we develop a greater sense of wholeness.

TEILHARD'S EXISTENTIAL DIALECTIC OF HAPPINESS

Teilhard is known for his revolutionary contributions bridging religion and science. One of his most pragmatic and applicable yet lesser-known ideas is his "existential dialectic of happiness." He presents this three-part formula as a model that we can effectively use in our lives. It is present in the work of Jung and Assagioli, as well. Beginning with Teilhard, we can use this formula to trace the connection between his vision with the psychoanalytic theories from Jung and Assagioli to explore how it can lead us to a more integral understanding of the fullness of life.

According to Teilhard, as life becomes more complex and as the human person becomes more conscious, the fulfillment that we seek is found in happiness: fully ourselves and fully alive. Teilhard's 1943 essay "Reflections on Happiness" suggests that happiness is the product of a life that is lived authentically and vibrantly. He outlines his "existential dialectic of happiness" in three steps, as follows:

> If we are to be fully ourselves and fully alive, we must:
>
> (1) be centered on ourselves;
> (2) be de-centered on the "other;"
> (3) be super-centered on one greater than ourselves...
>
> Not only physically, but intellectually and morally, we are only human if we develop ourselves.[13]

The first stage, *centration*, is our search for and development of personal autonomy. This is typically understood as having a "sense of self," or in psychological terms, the ego (our sense of *I*). Centration is fundamental within early childhood, when we learn a sense of individuality, first apart from our parents and then in a gradually wider social context.

Once our quest for personal autonomy has begun, we are empowered to expand outward, allowing us to encounter the "other." We meet the world outside of ourselves, and we can move beyond the "centered" notion of our identity. *Decentration* is a core element of early adulthood. At this time in life, we may enter several scenarios where we are taken beyond our own identity and enter into a wider field of awareness: Falling in love, heartbreak, injury, major achievement, and catastrophic failures or great losses are universal in their ability to move us beyond our initial sense of self.

Decentration, which Teilhard also calls *excentration*, adds "a nuance of drama and sorrow to the notion of extraction or separation."[14] In Teilhard's eyes, this is a "reversal" of sorts within evolution: "Ultimately, the world can only be joined to you, Lord, by a sort of inversion, turning inside out or excentration where not only individual success but even the appearance of all human progress must be temporarily overshadowed."[15] He calls it a reversal because evolution tends to demonstrate the union of elements. This is true; becoming decentered is contrary to uniting. Yet, this step is necessary for our awareness to grow beyond our own personal sense of unity. When we become decentered, we do not typically lose our sense of self. Rather, it is more like there is a diffusion of our awareness. What was once so concentrated on the self, known through centration, is now expanded to include a consideration of the other within our concept of unity.

We are now able to consciously extend beyond ourselves and encounter the "other" in a way that is not only conducive for our own survival but considers and works for the survival of the other as well. Teilhard writes, "By a sort of reversal towards the other its growth culminates in giving and in excentration."[16] First, we move into ourselves. Second, we move out of ourselves. We find our sense of center, and then we are moved beyond it.

Finally, *super-centration*, or what Teilhard also calls *hypercentration*, allows an awareness of our relationship within a collective being, within a union in consciousness. Therefore, Teilhard says that each element in a convergent universe is completed "by its incorporation within a higher pole of consciousness in which alone it can enter into contact with all the others."[17] This "higher consciousness" is not something otherworldly and available exclusively to sages and saints. First and foremost, it is within us. It is also within the other. It is within the world: within our planet Earth and within all the known and unknown vastness of the universe.

Thus, it is in the third stage of super-centration that we view ourselves in relation to the Whole. The Whole includes us, and it includes the other. The Whole includes the planet, and it includes the entire expanse of the universe. The Whole includes all that has been, all that is, and all that will be. The Whole is the cosmic center within which we live, and move, and have our being.

Centration, decentration, and super-centration: We find our identity, our identity is expanded in our encounter with other, and our individual identity and our relationship to other are held together in the Whole. Perhaps it can be seen even simpler as coming together, falling apart, and then being made new. When we are made new, we are not starting over yet integrating the processes of coming together and falling apart, re-creating our perspective so that we can become more aware of, and more authentically embody, the whole of the process.

While the fullness of life and happiness that we seek are ultimately found in our awareness of our relationship with the supercenter, or the Whole, it is only with our labor and our struggle in the initial and intermediate stages that the final stage of union is made possible. Furthermore, I would argue that having a sense of our relationship with the Whole does not magically alleviate the burdens and sufferings of the world or our awareness of them. If anything, awareness of our relationship with the Whole compels us to act by consciously immersing ourselves more deeply into matter and into the world. We are moved to take on not only the struggle and the suffering, but moreover to consciously embody the process that is unfolding within you, within me, within all people, and within all the world.

As we go forward, we will first explore Teilhard's work and vision. Then we will examine Teilhard in relation to Jung and Assagioli. Throughout each chapter, we will be returning to this formula and applying it to their work. I will take the liberty of applying it in a general sense to the work of each thinker, yet I do believe that it can be applied in other, more finely nuanced ways to their lives and to their thought. Beyond our application of the dialectic to the thought of Teilhard, Jung, and Assagioli, I would encourage you to consider how the existential dialectic has applied and applies to your own pursuit of a vibrant and authentic spiritual life.

CONSCIOUS EVOLUTION

As a boy growing up in south central France, Teilhard recalls seeking what he calls *le Tout* (*the All*), or an ultimate element of permanence at the core of creation. His fixation began with metals and then progressed to rocks. Eventually, he earned a doctorate in paleontology. However, it was not until Teilhard read Henri Bergson's 1907 *Creative Evolution* that he truly began to define what he was seeking in the Ultimate Element at the core of all things. He compared what he could see through science to be true from a traditional understanding of evolution, with the ideas proposed by Bergson that evolution is the result of a creative impulse that we as humans can consciously embody.

Evolution, according to Teilhard, is the ongoing and unfolding process of creation. Evolution reaches its apex in humanity's completion in the transcendent. Teilhard went beyond the traditional interpretation of creation as a singular act occurring at the beginning of time. Instead, he sees creation as a continual outpouring of Godself, as an evolutionary "system animated by an oriented and convergent movement."[18]

As a geologist, Teilhard possessed a tactile sense of the real. To separate his love of the world and his faith in God would be to deny the relationship between the two. Throughout his work, Teilhard tactfully weaves together his personal faith and his empirical understanding of the world. He realizes that God is not static. The God of evolution is dynamic, emerging, and becoming more consciously embodied through the human person.

In *The Divine Milieu*, Teilhard speaks of "the practical conviction that the universe, in the hands of the Creator, continues to be the clay in which he shapes numerous possibilities according to his will."[19] He understands life as fundamentally relational, whereas "to be" is to be in relationship.[20] Evolution is a process by which disparate elements come into union with one another. Despite living through periods of such rapid and tumultuous advances—especially in science, industry, and warfare—Teilhard understood the complexities of the modern world as indicating the emergence of a more unitive consciousness.

Evolution ascends by way of the material *complexification* of structures: quarks fusing to form nuclei, nuclei attracting electrons to form atoms, atoms seeking partners to form molecules, molecules forming polymers and, eventually, cells. Through complexification, Teilhard describes how there is a *without* and *within* to the stuff of the universe. The *without* is the physical makeup of matter: the protons, neutrons, and electrons making up atoms, the atoms making up molecules, and so on. The *within*, the psychic dimension of matter, is a *consciousness*.[21] We can understand the *within* as the attraction that draws and holds the difference parts of the *without* together. This attraction begins on the simplest levels of matter, even where there would not appear to be what we commonly might call "conscious." For example, we can agree that human beings, animals, and even plants, to a degree, possess a level of consciousness. Teilhard shows us that even rocks, dirt, and dust retain a small level of consciousness. There is an attraction that holds the dirt, the rocks, the trees, the water, the Earth, and the entire universe together.

The increase in material complexity leads to an increase in the amount of information being transferred between the different parts making up a structure, which leads to an overall increase in consciousness. We tend to acknowledge an organism is conscious when it appears "alive." Teilhard refers to consciousness as the "fundamental element, the very stuff of the real."[22] Complexity and consciousness drive each other, increasing mutually as evolution ascends. Teilhard uses the term *complexity-consciousness* to refer to the two in union with one another. We can certainly examine either complexity or consciousness on their own, yet Teilhard stresses how, like spirit and matter, complexity and consciousness are like two sides of the same coin.

Teilhard observes that "matter reveals the property of arranging itself in increasingly complex groups and, at the same time, in increasingly deeper levels of consciousness."[23] Consciousness, for Teilhard, is the same as spirit. He writes, "By spirit I understand 'the spirit of synthesis and sublimation' in which through constant trial and error is painfully concentrated the power of unity that is diffused in the universal multiple: spirit born within and as a function of matter."[24]

Teilhard's *Law of Complexity-Consciousness* describes the fundamental unity between spirit and matter. He sees that "a richer and better organized structure will correspond to the more developed consciousness."[25] Greater complexity means greater consciousness. Increased consciousness results in an expanded awareness of the spiritual nature of matter.

Our impulse toward higher forms of consciousness leads to a greater expression of our spirit. Teilhard writes, "Spirit is the goal towards which nature's age-long labors are directed... driven...by an urge towards a little more freedom, a little more power, more truth."[26] The Law of Complexity-Consciousness demonstrates how the higher levels of complexity produced in evolution result in higher levels of consciousness.

Teilhard says that the human person "represents the highest embryonic stage we know in the growth of spirit on Earth."[27] Kathleen Duffy explains that "human consciousness, due in part to the size and complexity of the human brain, is presently the most developed expression of matter's inner conscious face."[28] Teilhard's ability to see this conscious face allowed him a vision of how increased complexity-consciousness leads to greater unity.

Since we are evolution's most advanced unit of complexity-consciousness, our growth is essential for evolution's ascent. Our spiritual development is bound to our growth in consciousness. We have the capability for self-awareness so that we can continue evolution's ascent, but in a more sophisticated and personalized way. We are like the "new wine skins" that Jesus refers to, able to expand to contain the new spirit emerging within us. The universe is undergoing spiritualization on every level and is most remarkable in our human being.

Our bodies are made up of billions of cells unseen, yet they form the organs, systems, skin, and bones needed to express the totality of our beings. Grace perfects nature. Our physiological complexity is but one level of complexity within our being. The material complexity makes it possible for the noetic, or mental or psychic, content of our mind and spirit to come into being. Our species has unleashed a torrent of novelty unlike anything else seen in nature. Civilization, philosophy, religion, art, agriculture, architecture, dance, economics, politics, nanotechnology, artificial intelligence, and quantum technology all far surpass the complexity and the consciousness of an ant hill or a beehive.

Yet, there is a paradox present within our human systems. Our systems are more complex than those of the ants and bees. However, our human systems—including our physiological bodily systems along with our psychology and spirituality—tend to not be consciously integrated into the Whole. For example, our entrancement by screens has led to overexposure to blue light, which results in a disruption of the quality of our sleep and our circadian rhythms. Circadian rhythms are natural cycles that help to coordinate the biological systems of an organism for its overall wellness. Our overreliance and misuse of blue light–emitting screens, along with so many other components of modern life, have led us to an unhealthy disconnection from our biology.

Our systems that are dominant and paradigm defining tend to be centralized, or we might say "centered," as in the first stage of Teilhard's Existential Dialectic. We even refer to them, colloquially, as "Big Agriculture," "Big Oil," or "Big Tobacco." Some entities are even as looming as "the Military-Industrial Complex" or "the intelligence community." We are now living in the tension of transition from the first stage and into the second and third stages: *decentration* and *super-centration*. The three stages, while sequential, can coexist and be occurring simultaneously. As a very practical example, some of us may purchase our groceries from big box stores or large-scale commercial grocer franchises, who source their goods from a *centralized* global food corporation, like Cargill. Other people choose to shop at local farmers' markets, or perhaps even grow some of their own food and engage in a *decentralized* model of food. Our life operates on and within centralized and decentralized systems.

Let us finally consider the many exceptional people in the world who embody the Divine in a super-centered way. Without need for embellishment, we can acknowledge how they personify the faults and finitude of a human, while also being a vessel for a greater expression of God's Presence within the world. Every saint knows that they are a sinner, yet they live in a way that serves a bigger purpose. They live with a greater sense of the Whole and how they fit into it. To have a sense of the larger Whole, we need a sense of ourselves first, and then of the other. We must first live in the tension of becoming ourselves *and* encountering the other to enter a more conscious relationship with the Whole.

We are at a point now in our world where we are having collectively conscious experiences at an increased rate. This is the felt increase, or ascent, of complexity and consciousness. Looking back on collective experiences during my own lifetime, one that comes to mind is September 11, 2001, when the world had shared feelings of pain, anger, sadness, betrayal, and grief in wake of the terror attacks in the United States. In more recent years, the pandemic of 2020 was a global event that broadened our collective awareness of our need for connectivity and more integral solutions to complex and systemic problems. Troublesome as these events were, they resonated on a global scale, raising our awareness.

In the summer of 2023, people were seeking the "path of totality" of a solar eclipse. I was particularly sensitive to the language surrounding the total solar eclipse. I was floored by the seemingly universal usage of this terminology of "totality" and entertained its implications as possibly indicative of a collective awareness, albeit syntactically, of our movement toward the Whole.

Did this utterance come from a collective consciousness? Could this be a sign of the collective human organism waking up to our true spiritual identity as Divine children?

These questions are rhetorical, although another thing that stood out about the collective response to the eclipse was how the spirit around the event was much different than the attitude surrounding my first two examples of global events. In the same way that using the language of a "world war" holds an impending sense of doom for all, there is something about the use of the word *totality* that implies a spirit of hope and connection, even a sense of direction and a goal. In fact, the solar eclipse ended up being quite a celebratory occasion for the many people who traveled from their homes and made the pilgrimage to the various cities across the world where they could experience the ephemeralness of this celestial alignment. Through the matter making up our bodies and minds, our spirit yearns for wholeness and fullness, the totality we find as we follow evolution's path.

2

Following Evolution's Path

EVOLVING TO THE OMEGA POINT

Teilhard's book *The Phenomenon of Man* explains his theory that the universe is evolving in a specific direction, toward a point of completion. The book's preface opens with him giving a disclaimer that his work should not be read as a metaphysical reflection, nor as a theological essay, but as a "scientific treatise."[1]

Teilhard begins by tracing the increase in complexity and consciousness. He culminates with the arrival of the human and our capacity for self-reflection. Teilhard theorizes that the universe, through the human person—first as an individual, and then as a larger, collective whole—is evolving to a point of final and total unity in consciousness. While Teilhard does not seek to reconcile religion and science through *Phenomenon*, he is eventually led to a point where the science is best explained through religious terms.

The *Omega Point* is the goal and term of evolution—when complexity-consciousness reaches its ultimate expression. The

Omega Point is the natural point of convergence of humanity and the whole cosmos with God. Teilhard borrowed the word *Omega* from the final letter of the Greek alphabet, illustrating the fullness of Christ at the end of time—"the Alpha and the Omega, the first and the last, the beginning and the end" (Rev 22:13; cf. 1:8). According to Thomas King, Teilhard's use of the word *Point* implies "that the final end of the universe is centered and personal."[2]

Teilhard calls the Omega Point "a center different from all other centers because it 'super-centers' by assimilation; a personality distinct from all other personalities that it perfects by uniting with them."[3] All consciousness and all material complexity reaches a point of total union. The Omega Point is similar to the idea of the singularity popularized by Ray Kurzweil, where through technology there is a union in consciousness. Omega is a more integral form of union because it goes beyond technology to include the human heart and our capacity for a consciousness rooted in the foundational energies of love.

Teilhard explains four characteristics of the Omega Point:

1. Actual
2. Transcendent
3. Autonomous
4. Irreversible[4]

1. *Actual*: The lower forms of complexity and consciousness found throughout nature, especially those that exhibit social structures, are indicative of higher forms of complexity and consciousness within the world. The universal embodiment of complexity, consciousness, and socialization is the Omega Point. Socialization, union, and love are expressed on the simplest of levels of complexity. This would not be possible, according to Teilhard, if these qualities did not also exist on the highest of levels. The sense of wholeness and fulfillment

that we can consciously embody is a fractal of the universal wholeness. Omega is real and exists within the universe.

2. *Transcendent*: Omega, while within evolution, also transcends evolution; the Omega Point is both immanent and transcendent. Omega's otherworldliness can be likened to the concept of a strange attractor. Strange attractors are acausal and work in a fractal nature, showing "chaotic orbits" that "embody intricate yet unpredictable order."[5] We can't always explain why things happen through cause and effect. It is not always a "push" from causal events of the past that makes things happen. Sometimes, we find ourselves being "pulled" by a force in the future. This force could be as concrete as a goal, or as mysterious as an intuition. The universe, in its fullness, beckons every aspect within itself to grow and evolve toward its full potential as well.

3. *Autonomous*: Since Omega is transcendent, it is also free from the limitations of space and time; it is bound by neither locality nor temporality. Omega has always been present throughout time, yet Omega emerges in greater wholeness and clarity as we move into the future.

4. *Irreversible*: Omega's qualities of being actual, transcendent, and autonomous make it something that is both attainable and imperative—it must happen and cannot be undone. It is the inevitable product of an evolving universe.

Omega lives within us, and we live within Omega. It calls us, and all of creation, to evolve to our fullest state of being.

Consequently, Teilhard connects the Omega Point to Christ, in whom "all things hold together" (Col 1:17) and in whom "we live and move and have our being" (Acts 17:28). Teilhard sees the human person as a phenomenon because we are self-aware. The ultimate example of the human person in its fullness as this phenomenon of self-awareness is the risen Jesus, who passed through the process of birth, death, and resurrection.

The Omega Point is both the social and spiritual term of the earth because, through Christ Omega, there is a fullness of conscious relationship between humanity, the Divine, and all of evolution. This point of maximum complexity-consciousness is the fullness of the human person *and* a fullness of the human organism, now spiritually mature—a humanity divinized.

Here we can observe Teilhard's existential dialectic at play. The first two stages, centration and decentration, are present in the growth from the individual human person to the collective of humanity. The individual human person stands as the example of centration, where we gain a sense of self and identity. The human collective demonstrates the concept of decentration, where we encounter "other." We move beyond our individual sense of self and into a new sense of identity that exists in relationship to others. This disrupts the initial order of centration. While we explore this in the coming pages in further detail, we can rightly predict that these first two stages of centration and decentration will be super-centered in the Omega Point.

CHRIST'S COSMOTHEANDRIC BEING

When Christ entered evolution through the birth of Jesus of Nazareth, this Christified the entire universe with divinity. It was not as if, in a single moment, the universe was filled with Christ Consciousness because Jesus was born. Instead, we might suppose that Christ Consciousness first emerged in human form as the unbridled joy and total dependence of the baby born in a stable. Gradually, Christ Consciousness matured in its perfection over the scope of Jesus's life. We can even speculate that, before Jesus, the most protean seed of Christ Consciousness first emerged with the Big Bang. This is more theologically correct, in line with Logos, or the Word of

God, being the operating principle of reality. Jesus is understood as the Word made flesh.

The lesson is the same: Our spiritual growth is a journey. It is never a one-off moment in which we are completed and made whole; it is an unfolding over our entire life.

The other great message is that God is present throughout our journey. Christ is traditionally understood to possess a *hypostatic* being, or a nature that is fully human and fully divine. Teilhard identifies a larger identity of Christ with a third nature. In Christ's third nature, or Christ's *cosmic being*, God is present within all of the universe. Raimon Panikkar uses the word *cosmostheandric* to describe the total nature of Christ as Teilhard understands it. *Cosmostheandric* means that Christ's being is of the *cosmos* (*cosmos*), *God* (*theos*), and *humanity* (*andros*). God permeates all of reality and through our lives we can encounter God in conscious ways that lead the world to union. This results in the emergence of a higher, collective order within evolution—the Omega Point.

The Omega Point, or Christ Omega, incarnates within human history first by way of Jesus of Nazareth. Then, Teilhard writes, "once he has been raised to the position of Prime Mover of the evolutive movement of complexity-consciousness, the cosmic-Christ becomes cosmically possible."[6] Through the person (consciousness) of Christ, we can become aware of the powerful and transcendent energies that reveal themselves through evolution. Teilhard describes the emergence of the Omega Point as the dawn of *Christogenesis*: "For each one of us, every energy and everything that happens, is super-animated by his influence and [Christ's] magnetic power. To sum up, Cosmogenesis reveals itself...first as Biogenesis and then Noogenesis, and finally culminates in the Christogenesis which every Christian venerates."[7]

In the phase of Christogenesis, we begin to see "the possibilities of a universal Communion."[8] Our eyes are opened to "a

Christianity re-incarnated for the second time in the spiritual energies of Matter" and is "precisely the 'ultra-Christianity' we need now to meet the ever more urgent demands of the 'ultra-human.'"[9] The *ultra-human* is the "reality of an extension beyond the human."[10] We have a sense of what it means to be ultra-human through instances where we are "at our best." Psychologists study the *flow state* or higher level of performance, often embodied by experts of a skill who can make a difficult task look like effortless artwork. Additionally, theologian Karl Rahner wrote about the "plus dimension" in describing moments when we experience an extraordinary awareness of God's presence in our lives, or, more accurately, of our lives within the divine life of God.

Teilhard writes how ultra-humans are called to seek the "God of the Ahead." The God of the Ahead is different from the more traditional "God of the Above." The God of the Above is reminiscent of the "old man in the sky" who is purely transcendent and part of a detached cosmology. The God of the Ahead is more like the risen Christ encountered on the road to Emmaus. Over time, the disciples eventually become aware that the mysterious traveler who walks on the road with them is, in fact, Christ. In the context of evolution, our relationship with God calls us to be future-oriented. We do not ignore God's transcendence. Instead, we encounter God's transcendence through our conscious participation in evolution as it works toward its goal of union in Christ Omega.

The Cosmic Christ, the Omega Point of complexity-consciousness, draws us beyond our logical, thinking minds and grants us access to the fullness of our being by engaging our hearts. Spiritual growth takes us into a "love consciousness" where we have a greater awareness of our connectedness to all things. We do not throw away our rational, thinking minds, yet we transcend them with our hearts. By "*loving*, co-extensively and co-organically with all the past, the present and the future of a Universe which is in a process of centration upon itself,"[11] there is a greater emergence of the Cosmic Christ. The Cosmic Christ emerges more fully as we love more wholly.

Teilhard became aware of spirit and matter working in union. He saw that "the dualism in which [he] had hitherto been closed was disappearing like the mist before the rising sun. Matter and Spirit: these were no longer two things, but two states or two aspects of one and the same cosmic Stuff."[12] Christ's cosmic nature goes beyond the dual nature of Christ as God and human. It demonstrates a *panentheism*, where God is *within* all of created reality, all of the world.

"So true is this," writes Teilhard, "that to the 'informed eye' all opposition is blurred...between action and prayer, between centration upon self and excentration upon the Other."[13] To the trained eye, our daily actions can be offerings of service to the goal of Omega. The simplest of our daily activities can be small steps closer to God.

THE BODY OF CHRIST: THE CENTER OF EVOLUTION

The term *the Body of Christ* is central to Christianity. Teilhard might describe the Body of Christ as evolution's great work, its magnum opus. In Teilhard's perspective, evolution is a process of becoming. The Cosmic Christ is also in a state of emergence over time. Teilhard affirms three points about the concept of the Body of Christ that show us what its emergence looks like:[14]

The first is the realness of the Body-Person of Jesus: Jesus of Nazareth was a real person, flesh and blood, who lived among other humans on the planet Earth. This teaches us that Christ Consciousness is incarnate.

Second, the Body-Person here and now forms a personal Center for humankind and the material world: Jesus's realness establishes a point of connection (a "personal Center") between God and humanity, and thus between God and all creation. This teaches us that Christ Consciousness permeates reality.

Third, this personal Center is a physical Center: Jesus (the Divine) is our personal Center and lives in us! The more we live in Christ Consciousness, the Parousia becomes a more embodied reality. This teaches us that we, through Christ Consciousness, can see God in everything.

Christ begins centered in the person of Jesus. Then, Christ is decentered and becomes a personal Center beyond the person of Jesus. Finally, we evolve to become more Christ-like.

In *The Phenomenon of Man*, Teilhard says, "As early as in St. Paul and St. John, we read that to create, to fulfill, and to purify the world is, for God, to unify it by uniting it organically with himself."[15] The incarnation is part of evolution, not a static event. Through the human person of Jesus, the incarnation reaches an expressive point of dominion over time and space:

> How does [Christ] unify [creation]? By partially immersing himself in things, by becoming an element and then, from this vantage point in the heart of matter, assuming control and leadership of what we now call evolution. Christ, principal universal vitality because sprung up as a man among men, put himself in the position (maintained ever since) to subdue under himself, to purify, to direct and to give supernatural life to the general ascent of consciousness into which he inserted himself. By a continual act of communion and sublimation, he incorporates into himself the total psychism of the earth....He invests himself organically with the very majesty of his creation.[16]

Jesus lived, died, and rose from the dead. This same paradigm plays out in the cycle of our own lives through the process of centration, decentration, and super-centration. We are called, personally and universally, to become more Christ-like.

If we consider all of humanity stretched over history as a Body-Person, we might see the development of different parts of our being. Let us consider the pantheon of Hinduism as containing the sacred archetypes of the human psyche, amassing in a semblance of a collective ego. Gautama Buddha, in his attainment of enlightenment, can serve as a marker for the awakening of the evolving "mind" of humanity. Jesus, who can be considered a "love mystic," might designate the emerging "heart" of the collective human person, where the collective ego is transformed. Psychologist Thomas Legere observes how Jesus was neither "bottom-up" nor "top-down" in his spirituality, but love first:

> He did not take the Hindu approach of starting the spiritual journey at the "chakra" (or center of consciousness) having to do with security, and working one's way up from there. Nor did he take the approach of starting with higher states of consciousness and allowing those states to "filter down." Granted, his personal prayer, the "Lord's Prayer" does seem to do this, but, in the context of his whole life, he seems to have taken the approach that we need to begin by opening up the heart to others. Love one another unconditionally, totally, without judgment, forgiving seventy times seven, and your spiritual growth will take care of itself.[17]

Buddha's enlightened mind of the East and Jesus's loving heart of the West coming into union indicate how the world's different spiritual paths share converging trajectories. Their union demonstrates a growing wholeness within humanity as evolution moves toward a state of completion in Omega.

This analogy of the mind and heart of evolution may be

helpful in unpacking what Teilhard means when he references the Body-Person of Jesus as a "personal" and "physical" Center. The Body-Person of Jesus is how evolution embodies a personal and conscious relationship to the Divine. The "form" that this consciousness takes as Body-Person is crystalized in the person of Jesus by way of human consciousness. This allows us to be collectively transformed in recapitulatory fashion.

God is alive within our bodies made of matter, and God is alive in our consciousness, or spirit. Christopher Mooney observes that "whatever meaning 'physical' is to have...it will have to be situated in the realm of the human and the personal."[18] Our human experience can be united in many ways, yet a universal point of connection is our yearning for fullness and wholeness.

HUMAN CONVERGENCE IN THE COSMIC CHRIST

Teilhard observes how the Cosmic Christ emerges through two phases: the cosmic (natural) and the *Christic* (supernatural). The *cosmic* phase is the natural dilation of Christ through fullness of his Presence on a local level (within the Body-Person of Jesus of Nazareth). The *Christic* phase is a "final psychic center of universal concentration."[19] The Christic is "psychic" in the sense that it exists as a conscious state of being. Teilhard says the Christic is the "focal point of spiritual radiation concentrated by two thousand years of history in this place: today, it is here that we find the christic pole of the earth; it is here that the ascending axis of hominization is to be found."[20] The Christic is a supernatural process because it is the point at which we awaken to our spiritual connection to the world.

Like many components of Teilhard's thought, the cosmic and the Christic work together in a sequential yet simultaneous fashion. Teilhard recalls his revelation of the two phases in union:

> The cosmic sense and the christic sense: these two axes were born in me quite independently of one another, it would seem, and it was only after a long time and a great deal of hard work that I finally came to understand how, through and beyond the Human, the two were linked together, converged upon one another, and were in fact one and the same.[21]

Teilhard says the result of the cosmic and Christic phases is a *Person*. What he means is that the result of evolution is the expression of a Divine Personality. We can consider it like this:

> The universe has a body: the physical world of matter.
> The universe has a mind: the mental world of the noosphere.
> The universe has a spirit that is personal as God became human in the *person* of Jesus.

Jesus was more than his physical body and more than the information in his mind. He had a personality through which he related to others and interacted with the world.

From evolution there emerges an ultimate Personality (or Person) made up of all the personalities of human persons. When we evolve to a spiritual consciousness of the union of all things, we become aware of our place in that union. Our spiritual evolution demands our participation, in some form, within a larger community or context. When we are living authentically and with a sense of connection, our personality is usually at its best. Despite our lives being challenging, we can still live vibrantly and with purpose. In this same way, when we live authentic and connected lives, we participate in spiritualizing the universe by contributing to the emergence of Christ's total Personality through the gift of our own genuine personality.

Complexity-consciousness ascends through time and finds itself in conscious union within us. Through our human person, we become the emergence point for the "spiritualization" of matter. Spiritual life, or what Teilhard call the process of *spiritualization*, is an evolution in itself. Matter is in process of spiritualization. So are our spiritual lives. We are being continually being called to encounter God in new ways. We are always in process.

Spiritualization can be seen as a "metamorphosis not by dissociation of matter through an ascesis of separation but by transformation of matter through the actualization of its latent spiritual power."[22] Christ's injection into matter as a human sends a resonance throughout the entire universe that grows over time and space in "a movement that carries us forward....Hence our evidence that, from a purely scientific and experimental point of view, the real name of 'spirit' is 'spiritualization.'"[23] Thus, human expression is a highly spiritualized expression of matter.

Cosmic history appears to be a history of "spirit through matter." We observe matter become more collectively self-aware and expressive of its inner world. In this great unfolding of spirit-matter over the course of space and time, the Christ who holds all together is present and actualized within each of us individually. Moreover, Christ is actualized in a collective expression through our unification. The collective and emergent whole is a structure richer in complexity-consciousness than the smaller parts that comprise its structure. As the different parts converge with one another and we become aware of our place within the larger whole, a more holistic reality begins to form, both for us as individuals as well as for all of humanity.

"SEEING" THE WAY AHEAD

St. Hippolytus emphasizes that the transformative power of the total Christ is within all of humanity and is "available to anyone who comes to know his or her own soul."[24] He stresses the proverb "Know thyself" is an inclination to "discover God within thyself, for He has formed thee after His own image."[25] When St. Paul says, "It is no longer I who live, but it is Christ who lives in me" (Gal 2:20) he is referring to a transformation of consciousness and resonance with a greater being than his individual self. Teilhard teaches that only through an increase of consciousness can evolution advance to produce the emergence of higher structures and higher ways of being. These perspectives call us to look *inside* and find the Christ *within*. Teilhard's work, particularly his exposition of the Omega Point, is a testament to the inner journey for the sake of more unity in the world.

Teilhard expresses his progressive understanding of unitive consciousness in a way that is personal and unique to him. As a paleontologist, he sees the world in a rather exclusive way. His perspective as a scientist, along with his proclivity for visionary experiences, make his writing rather layered at times. Teilhard read William James's *The Varieties of Religious Experience* and Richard Maurice Bucke's *Cosmic Consciousness*.[26] Such works, along with his own experiences, exposed Teilhard to "the long procession of initiates given to the vision and worship of the All."[27] In this position, he clings to his *vision*. He realizes the importance of the gift of being able to pierce beyond the surface and into the heart of things where we encounter the Divine in the act of *seeing*:

> *Seeing*. One could say that the whole of life lies in seeing—if not ultimately, at least essentially. To be more is to be more united—and this sums up and is the very conclu-

> sion of the work to follow. But unity grows, and we will affirm this again, only if it is supported by an increase of consciousness, of vision. That is probably why the history of the living world can be reduced to the elaboration of ever more perfect eyes at the heart of a cosmos where it is always possible to discern more. Are not the perfection of an animal and the supremacy of the thinking being measured by the penetration and power of synthesis of their glance? To try to see more and to see better is not, therefore, just a fantasy, curiosity, or a luxury. See or perish. This is the situation imposed on every element of the universe by the mysterious gift of existence. And thus, to a higher degree, this is the human condition.[28]

Teilhard makes it very clear that our consciousness is key to a fulfilled human existence. His mystical vision provides us with an invaluable map of how the individual and the collective can work toward wholeness amid the complexity of the twenty-first century and the unknown future that awaits us. Teilhard experienced wholeness by encountering God through the world. Exploring his vision in the chapter to come reveals ways that his dynamic spirituality can empower us to grow in our relationship with the Divine.

3

Teilhard's Inner Journey

SEEING AS TEILHARD SEES

When Teilhard connected the Omega Point of evolution with the risen Christ, he wrote that his world lit up like "an explosion of dazzling flashes."[1] This discovery filled him with the spirit of hope that he embodied over his lifetime, despite facing continuous challenges, struggles, and even suffering. Fortunately for us, Teilhard wrote about his mystical experiences frequently and intimately. His mystical writings provide further clarity of his vision explained in the previous chapter. Even more importantly, Teilhard's mysticism allows us to enter into his spirit of hope and encounter God in a personal way.

I use the language of "seeing" God very intentionally. The previous chapter concluded with Teilhard's admonition that we must "see or perish." Teilhard does not mean that we must literally see God with our eyes or in a visionary experience where neurological stimuli might be triggering something classifiable as a visual hallucination; rather, we must have a larger sense of being, a vision of how we are related to the whole. Therefore, as we work through his mystical vision that he lays out so neatly, we will see how Teilhard refers to the varieties of ways that he experiences the Divine within the world. Whether it be through his senses or through his cognitive processing and reasoning, Teilhard's articulation of how he encounters the Divine in the world is likely to resonate with readers on some level.

As a Christian mystic who was also an accomplished scientist, Teilhard's "claim is that in the very act of scientifically achieving, he knew God."[2] While his writing is rather systematic, he writes of experiencing a mystical sense of intimacy with God. Thomas King understands Teilhard's mysticism as a mysticism of *knowing*, "for when human knowledge is in process, God is found in the act of knowing."[3] The more Teilhard learned about himself, others, and the world, the more he knew about God. Both research and prayer can move us from the darkness of unknowing into the light of knowing. Teilhard's work as a scientist and priest allowed these two paths to flow together in synthesis quite fluidly for him.

The end goal of Teilhard's mysticism is not simply union with the Divine. Instead, Teilhard's journey leads him to encounter a God known through relationship, interconnectivity, and interdependence. Therefore, Teilhard's mysticism is not only a passive intimacy within God's life, but an active and participatory union with the Divine in all things.

Teilhard shares his visionary experiences over the course of several works, most notably in *The Heart of Matter*, *The Divine Milieu*, and essays collected in *Writings in Time of War*, as well in personal letters to friends. In an early essay titled "The Mystical Milieu,"[4] Teilhard writes about five mystical circles:

1. Presence
2. Consistence

3. Energy
4. Spirit
5. Person

Teilhard's circles can be seen as concentric, with the first mystical circle he experienced, Presence, the largest and widest, with the other four circles fitting within it. Ultimately, all circles are centered on the fifth circle, the Circle of Person. It may also be helpful to imagine these concentric circles as spiraling up the side of a cone. The Circle of Presence is the "base" of the spiral, which becomes more tightly wound as it reaches its apex in the Circle of Person. Teilhard started broadly, sensing God's presence in the world. Over time, he became more focused on all the ways the Divine permeated his life. The wholeness Teilhard experienced because of his vision transformed him to the point where he could, near the end of his life, share with a friend, "I really feel that now I'm always living in God's presence."[5]

THE CIRCLE OF PRESENCE

Teilhard was a committed scientist, and his passion for discovery was "his way of touching what he sensed was animating and directing everything."[6] He sensed that there was something "more" to be discovered in creation, yet his love for the earth also persisted. He experienced a heightened awareness, which revealed to him the reality of a Divine Presence in matter, a "diffused radiance" that grew "more fragrant, more colored, more intense."[7] This new mystical sense enhanced the way Teilhard perceived creation. As his "inner world became luminous,"[8] Teilhard became accustomed to this new awareness that was stimulated by his scientific knowledge of the physical world; for his scientific vision provided him with what he needed to attempt to articulate his insights.

As a geologist, his eyes were naturally drawn to the landscape. He wrote about the way the sun's "deep brilliance"[9] seemed to make "the whole surface of things sparkle."[10] Teilhard's experience took on the form of sensory stimulation. Through the heightened awareness of his senses, he was able to perceive the presence of a higher unity within the world around him. Kathleen Duffy suggests that "Teilhard's sensitivity to light and color opened another pathway to the Divine Presence,"[11] like a visual portal.

Teilhard's close friends and colleagues witnessed his talent for observation, and recall how he "recognized Paleolithic artifacts with an uncanny sort of instinct,"[12] as "his downcast eyes would spot the smallest bit of cut stone betraying itself by its redness on the bare grayness of wind-swept soil."[13] Teilhard was incredibly observant while experiencing enhanced encounters with Presence. He speaks of how the radiance of Presence caused him to see "the play of colors on a transparent bubble"[14] and how "at other times, a crown of light seemed to surround everything and disclose the unique essence of the universe."[15] Surely, this aspect of Teilhard's visionary capacity helped him to experience things that others might not.

Through the Presence he experienced in nature, Teilhard saw how the world was illuminated by Divine Light: "This light is not the superficial glimmer...nor is it the violent flash which destroys objects and blinds our eyes. It is the calm and powerful radiance engendered by the synthesis of all the elements of the world."[16]

Teilhard also used the analogy of sound to describe Divine Presence: "I would like to...translate as faithfully as possible what I hear murmuring in me like a voice or a song which are not of me, but of the World in me."[17] He heard a "note which makes the whole World vibrate"[18] with "a vibration that passes all description, inexhaustible in the richness of its tones and notes, interminable in the perfection of its unity."[19]

He describes the unity of matter and spirit he experienced in his auditory encounter:

> All the sounds of created being are fused, without being confused, in a single note which dominates and sustains them...so all the powers of the soul begin to resound in response to its call; and these multiple tones, in their turn, compose themselves into a single, ineffably simple vibration in which all the spiritual nuances—of love and ecstasy, of passion and of indifference, of assimilation and of surrender, of rest and of motion—are born and pass and shine forth.[20]

Furthermore, Teilhard's study of physics would have allowed him an understanding of harmony and "how the human ear is trained and how the mind is psychologically conditioned to respond to certain harmonies, to certain combinations of tones that work well together."[21] He was aware that there was a divine dynamic within the brilliance that he observed in the world. As a result, he was opened to a new dimension in life that stimulated a desire to become one with the universe. The Presence that Teilhard sensed in the world spurred "an insatiable desire to maintain contact...with a sort of universal root of being."[22]

The first level of Teilhard's mysticism relies heavily on the body's senses. Our senses are often the first line through which the Divine Presence penetrates our mundane awareness and opens us up to the sacred in the world. We may not have a literal visionary experience in which we experience sensory phenomena. We may not need to. In and through our bodies we can accept, appreciate, and adore the sacred. This is very much the epitome of the phenomenon of the human person: We are the universe consciously experiencing itself.

THE CIRCLE OF CONSISTENCE

Teilhard's pursuit of the Divine took him beyond Presence into the mystical Circle of Consistence. Sounds, sights, and other sensations all indicated a greater presence within the world, but they did not totally fulfill Teilhard's yearning. Teilhard was seeking "an ultimate Element in which all things find their definitive consistence."[23] He was yearning to encounter the element that was permanent and could hold all other elements together. As a young man, he looked to the theory of gravity. He held in his heart the belief that, as scripture says, it is Christ "in [whom] all things hold together" (Col 1:17), yet he was perpetually challenged to comprehend this concept in a real and tangible way. He found himself inspired to look out into the cosmos. He began delving into the realms where, only today, in the twenty-first century, have astrophysicists begun understanding the origins of cosmogenesis and the mysterious forces that govern the universe.

In Teilhard's time, technologies were just beginning to give rise to the powerful tools used by scientists today. Though researchers nowadays might be closer to answering questions of cosmic consistency, the data is still challenging. It is currently theorized that only 4 to 5 percent of the cosmic density is attributable to ordinary matter. Another 25 percent of the cosmic density is believed to be dark matter, "a little understood entity that is probably composed of as-yet-unknown exotic subatomic particles that hold the galaxies together gravitationally but do not interact with light."[24] Dark matter is maintained to be central to the formation of cosmic structures such as galaxies. The remaining 70 percent of cosmic density is due to dark energy, which behaves like a reverse gravity, causing a speeding up in the expansion of the universe. What constitutes the elusive dark energy is still unknown.[25] "The precise makeup of dark matter and dark energy is one of the major open questions in astrophysics,"[26] writes Duffy.

The discoveries made via astrophysics help to comprehend the origin and scale of the cosmos. However, much of the universe and what makes it up remains a mystery. The unknown can be a catalyst for inspiration for scientists and seekers alike. At an early age, Teilhard became aware of the reality that things wither and die with impermanence. This troubled him, yet it also fueled his quest for permanence.

Duffy observes, "As [Teilhard] considered the immensity of the cosmos and the fragility of living things, his initial response was to assume that, since living things fall apart, he mattered little."[27] However, he began to appreciate the diversity of living organisms in the biosphere. He saw that, on one hand, "this crumbling away, which is the mark of the corruptible and the precarious, is to be seen everywhere." At the same time, on the other hand, "everywhere there are traces of, and a yearning for, a unique support, a unique and absolute soul, a unique reality in which other realities are brought together in synthesis."[28] Teilhard grew to see himself as a part of an interconnected and interdependent reality, as part of the life of the earth. As a result, his perspective expanded, and he gained a new vantage point for viewing himself in relation to the cosmos.

Teilhard began to see that the consistency he was seeking was not to be found in outward appearances or elements, but in what holds this intricately delicate union together. The Divine Presence that Teilhard experienced in the first circle gained a new power for Teilhard as he became aware of "the unifying influence of the universal Presence."[29] Now that he had come to see that the Divine was holding everything together, Teilhard yearned to become one with the universe so that he might be one with the Divine.

When I think of how I personally understand and apply the idea of a mystical Circle of Consistence, I do not typically think about gravity, dark matter, or dark energy. While I can certainly appreciate the magnitude of this kind of understanding of the universe, I do not have a workable grasp on the science behind any of it. What I *do* think of, regarding Divine Consistence, is the relationship between my experiences and the things I *do* know about. For example, as a theologian, I cannot help but approach, engage, and analyze my lived experience in the context of my background in theology and ministry. Another example: In having operated retreat centers, along with facilitating and participating in retreats, I find myself drawn to a deeper awareness of dynamics that apply to other areas in life such as the layout of space, a warm sense of hospitality, or the flow of a program.

As a final example, I think of my garden. Without a doubt, I have by now established a conscious connection with the beauty of the plants and the healthy and delicious fruit of their harvest. I am not going to say that I am some kind of nature mystic, yet I cannot look at my garden, or my chickens, or a tree, or an ocean and *not* be reminded of the sheer, Divine brilliance all around us, within us, and within the natural world. However, the more intimately I get involved with, and thus enter a relationship with the garden, I also foray into deeper complexity. Composting, soil science, plant propagation, food preservation, pollinators, and pest control have now become subjects for me to study and integrate into a more conscious gardening practice. Within each new instance of increased complexity is the birthing of an increase in consciousness. There is a new dimension and a new way in which to know God.

THE CIRCLE OF ENERGY

In the first mystical circle, Teilhard became conscious of the Divine Presence in the world. In the second circle, he was captivated by the Divine Consistence holding everything in the universe together. As Teilhard sought to unite with the Divine Consistence of the cosmos, Presence and Consistence now began to reveal themselves as Divine Energy. Through Teilhard's awareness of the structure and the properties of the universe, he started to see the incendiary energy that filled the cosmos.

Teilhard was now aware of his place within a cosmic structure that was alive with dynamic energy. Ilia Delio writes how "Teilhard reflected on the primordial reality of energy and the physical world of mass-energy where there is an inherent force of attraction within all dimensions of cosmic life."[30] As a paleontologist and mystic, Teilhard possessed what seems to be a panoramic, almost wide-angle perspective. He could envision the entire history of the planet while gazing over a landscape and contemplating its growth. Despite his study of sedentary rocks and bones, Teilhard was able to envision the dynamic processes that had shaped and moved matter. Teilhard experienced what Duffy calls a "fast-forwarded view of Earth's more than four-billion-year history" that "highlighted Earth's profound fluidity and plasticity" and was convinced of "the validity of the theory of evolution but also [of] its creative potential."[31]

This newfound appreciation for evolution allowed Teilhard to see how over four billion years of life on earth was evolving to more complex forms. Teilhard recognized that over time, the union of simpler structures would reveal the emergence of more complex structures. Duffy asserts, "A thrust towards union seems to be coded into the very fabric of the cosmos. On each level of the cosmic hierarchy, a process exists that tends to create new entities."[32] This describes the theory that Teilhard calls creative union. As Teilhard experienced the Divine Energy in the complexity of his life, he understood our duty to "test every barrier, try every path, plumb every abyss"[33] to find our place in the cosmos. Teilhard's view of the cosmos became "dynamic and organic,"[34] revealing a universe alive, vibrant, filled with Divine Energy, and enduring.[35]

Teilhard began his mystical journey by observing the radiance of the Divine Presence throughout creation. He persisted in his search for the Divine in matter, leading to his discovery of the Divine Consistence that brings creation into union. Teilhard pressed on and he eventually uncovered a dynamic Divine Energy at work in the universe. Divine Energy allowed Teilhard an understanding of suffering and evil. He saw them as the natural products of an unfinished world, the price we must pay to live, to enjoy freedom, and to grow.[36] Duffy writes how "the emergence of new structures is often accompanied by violent processes: simple nuclei collide silently and form more complex nuclei; supernovas explode to provide rich material for future planetary systems; volcanoes erupt and cause devastation, yet eventually the soil becomes quite fertile."[37] Thus, Teilhard recognized the teleological value of suffering (having a goal or purpose). He was no longer afraid to become one with the universe, even if this meant he must take on the sufferings of the cosmos. As Teilhard continued to learn how the Divine Energy was moving in the universe, he grew in awareness that human action has "a universal, absolute, value....Its aim is...to channel...*the whole* of the World's drive towards the Beautiful and the Good."[38] He understood this responsibility as his own, having faith that his own effort would be sufficient in working with Divine Energy.

Teilhard understood that his life and actions were part of a larger cosmic endeavor. Therefore, he viewed his work as sacred work. Whether he was acting as a priest, a paleontologist, or any other role he found himself in, Teilhard saw the act of being in harmony with Divine Energy as a sacred duty. Teilhard's integration of the Divine Presence, Divine Consistence, and Divine Energy demonstrates how he was growing through each of the mystical circles, using what he had learned from the previous circles to develop a more coherent understanding of God. The Presence called Teilhard forth to encounter the ubiquity of

Divine Consistence, which ultimately positioned him to embrace the universe through working in union with its current of growth and transformation.

As a paleontologist, Teilhard's attunement to the rhythms of the earth over its ancient history allowed him a keen sense of the ebb and flow of Divine Energy within the world. His own life was a series of challenges and struggles. Teilhard embraced the complexity of matter, of the world, and of his own life. Though he was confronted with steady resistance, he still ascended to a greater awareness of God. There are plenty of books available that offer practices for heightening our sensitivity to energy and how we can more consciously tap into its movement through our lives and in the world for the sake of growth and connection. What I feel is most valuable from Teilhard's mystical understanding of Divine Energy is the consideration of how our actions contribute to the larger work of evolution. Our everyday lives can be offerings to the Divine. By blessing our work, we deepen our awareness of how it is, in some way, a sacred task that contributes to evolution's goal. We gain a sense of how it nurtures the growth and emergence of the embodied love and union of the Omega Point.

Currently serving as the director of the Spirituality and Retreat Center at Daylesford Abbey, my job duties vary greatly depending on the season, the day, the hour, or the minute. One afternoon, over lunch, I was talking about an administrative task I was involved in earlier that morning. It had to have been a monotonous task, because Fr. Andrew Ciferni, a Norbertine canon at the abbey, teasingly asked me with a smile, "And what does this have to do with the building up of the Omega Point?"

Tedious as our lives may be at times, they still move toward a goal. Through an awareness of Divine Energy, we can better embrace the ebb and flow of movement toward a larger purpose or sense of completion in our own lives, even if it is in the small and simple tasks that move the day along and contribute to a larger mission, cause, or project. We will all leave our mark on evolution, we will all have contributed in some way. Even if the fruit of our labor is not harvested within our lifetimes, we can still do the work that is necessary now in areas big and small to help create a better future. Beyond our actions, and perhaps most important, is the intention we fuse into our work and the disposition with which we act, infusing matter with our conscious spirit. The Omega Point emerges from the collective where each element is doing its part to contribute toward the overall dynamic of union.

THE CIRCLE OF SPIRIT

As Teilhard pursued Divine Energy and its presence within his own life, he journeyed deeper into the heart of the universe and into the heart of God. He was captivated by the expanding and evolving universe and the fact that he was a part of this process. Furthermore, he was now aware that the universe was evolving *through* his being. Charged with Divine Energy, Teilhard directed his focus inward to explore the current of Creative Union and to see how it was working in his own story:

> And so, for the first time in my life perhaps (although I am supposed to meditate every day!), I took the lamp and, leaving the zone of everyday occupations and relationships where everything seems clear, I went down into my inmost self, to the deep abyss whence I feel dimly that my power of action emanates. But as I moved further and further away from the conventional certainties by which social life is superficially illuminated, I became aware that I was losing contact with myself.[39]

In the Circle of Spirit, Teilhard encountered what Thomas King calls the "world dwelling within us...the spirit of the

Earth...[that is] apart from our conscious mind and often acts independently of our conscious decisions."[40] As Teilhard's awareness shifted into his inner world, he described a plurality of consciousness: "At each step of the descent a new person was disclosed within me of whose name I was no longer sure and who no longer obeyed me."[41]

Teilhard was challenged by this pluralistic spirit of the earth, yet he came to learn through it that an isolated human soul is not capable of seeing God. Instead, union with the Divine requires the effort of the soul united to all the other souls.[42] He writes, "Our individual mystical effort awaits an essential completion in its union with the mystical efforts of all other men."[43] Teilhard saw that, just as the elements are attracted to form a union, so is the spirit of the earth. Seeking union, Teilhard explored more deeply: "And when I had to stop my exploration because the path faded from beneath my steps, I found a bottomless abyss at my feet, and out of it came—arising I know not from where—the current which I dare to call *my* life."[44]

As Teilhard moved into his inner world, he found himself traveling back in time. The line of delineation that separated his person from the rest of the universe virtually disappeared, as he traced his personal cosmic history. Duffy writes that "as he descended back through the eons of time, the landscape became less and less familiar...until...finally, near the beginning of time, all cosmic structure dissolved into a sea of elementary particles."[45] Until this point, Teilhard had been encountering God within the richness of the world. However, this experience was revealing a world to Teilhard that was much less structured and much less complex. This point in deep time lacked the vibrancy of the Presence, Consistence, and Energy that had been alluring Teilhard forward on his journey. Teilhard's downward trajectory in this experience of traveling back through time was not a step backward on his spiritual path. Instead, this was a necessary descent into matter so that he could continue his exploration into the Divine.

Thomas King calls this pivotal moment Teilhard's "reversal":

> After [Teilhard's] reversal he would identify with the tense and rising current of life, the current known as evolution. Evolution is seen as a movement away from dissolution and into ever more complex structures; it is a movement to consciousness and freedom, to "absolute fuller being." These two movements, one that would relax into dissolution and nothingness and the other that would struggle towards greater complexity and being, underlie all of Teilhard's thought.[46]

As Teilhard reversed his descent and ascended in the direction of greater complexity, he became aware that all convergent elements within the universe give rise not only to greater complexity, but also to greater consciousness. In the Circle of Spirit, Teilhard came to see the evolutionary cosmos as "a single organic object."[47] He describes the universe as "an interdependent mass of infinitesimal centers structurally interconnected by their conditions of origin and their development."[48] The more matter evolves in complexity, it develops a greater capacity to embody spirit, or consciousness. This mystical circle allowed Teilhard an awareness of how the spirit of the earth was also the spirit in the core of his own being. At this point in his journey, he came to see how God can be known beyond the Presence perceived in nature, and beyond the Consistence of the universe. He understood that the Divine penetrates reality even further, serving as the Energy that unites. Teilhard recognized that a rise in consciousness is a rise in the spiritualization of the universe, thus a greater awareness and expression of the Divine Spirit.

Teilhard identifies humans as representing "the highest embryonic stage we know in the growth of spirit on Earth."[49] With our capacity for higher levels of consciousness, we possess "a naturally advantageous panoramic point."[50] Therefore, the unity of mind that forms the noosphere allows for an even higher level of consciousness, one that is collective and focused. The modern age, according to Teilhard, has expressed a great individualism—the opposite of unity. However, the noosphere is conscious of itself and capable of collaboration, of spiritual relationship, and of sympathy, and thus of counteracting the dissolution brought on by individualism.[51]

The noosphere is embedded within all the other layers of the earth. Teilhard describes the noosphere as "a vast nervous system"[52] that results in a collective brain.[53] Thus, the state of the noosphere is "an external indication of another far more fundamental work that is taking place: the inner psychic organization of the noosphere."[54] Therefore, the social, political, and economic connections that encircle the globe are all expressive of the status of the collective of individual minds that aggregate to form its existence.[55] Though the noosphere is a product of billions of years of evolution, it is also the producer of greater consciousness. It serves the function of directing consciousness toward a goal.[56]

Teilhard became aware of the Divine Spirit that fills all things and animates matter. Inspired by the intuition that relationship is central to evolution, Teilhard sought to identify this dynamic in the world. He reflects that "to be more is more fully to unite more."[57] Duffy writes, "The one who is fully alive then is creative and innovative...relates to the other...draws together persons, places, and things, as well as information and knowledge from whatever is available in the environment."[58] Through his longing to become one with the universe, Teilhard was also expanding and enhancing the ways that he was in relationship with the world around him.

Relationship allows us to become "spiritually stronger and more conscious."[59] In reflecting upon this overarching dynamic, Teilhard was moved to see himself and each human as unique parts in the evolutionary process. He was able to appreciate his role as part of humanity and part of the cosmos. Having experienced a sense of oneness with the universe, Teilhard felt a new impetus to participate in the creative and dynamic unfolding of evolution toward greater consciousness and being *more*: "To your all-embracing providence...I shall respond by my care never to miss an opportunity of rising 'towards the level of spirit.'"[60]

The drive within the cosmos to become more calls *us* to become more. Evolution needs our mind with its ability to think, and it needs our heart with its ability to love. Love was the name that Teilhard gave to the immense energy that collected and condensed in the Circle of Spirit. In his mission to *be more* and play his part in evolution, he continued to pursue this radiant cosmic love and wondered where it might take him. He knew that as he increased the ways that he was in relationship with the universe, he would grow closer to God.

The mystical Circle of Spirit calls us to an awareness of unity and how we are held together by a power greater than our own. When we intentionally and consciously engage life and all its complexity, we commonly begin to feel a pull toward other like-minded people who are engaged in similar ways. We share a common Spirit.

Teilhard experienced this comradery through his encounter with the spirit of the earth. Spirit allowed him to see that, to experience a sense of fullness and wholeness of his being, he could not simply merge with the earth as a surrender of his being. Instead, he saw how a fuller devotion of his being would be to *rise* with evolution to higher states of consciousness. This required that he begin to go beyond himself, and, beyond his limited connection through only his own being to the world.

Now, Teilhard found himself uniting with the world through a more integral sense of being, in a wider sense of relationship in *other*.

The pragmatic lesson from the intensity of Teilhard's mystical sense of Spirit is that we are all in evolution together. Evolution is also within us. We need each other. As we encounter other, we eventually enter various kinds of socialization and, through relationship, we emerge within a higher state of being. We can embrace the flow of Divine Energy and let it move us into a larger sense of being within a community of Spirit. As we live within these chaotic times, we can challenge ourselves and each other to become aware of how we are being called to new ways of seeing and embodying love, union, authenticity, and fullness in our lives.

THE CIRCLE OF PERSON

The final mystical circle Teilhard entered was the Circle of Person. In this circle, he sought to encounter the God who was rising to greater expression through the spiritual power of matter. The Circle of Spirit unveiled the power to unite within as a community. There was a "body" forming from the unity of human energy as expressed through the spirit of the earth. As Teilhard's vision of the Divine came into focus, he was able to see that within evolution, there was also a "face."

A personality was emerging from the convergence of all of the other personalities making up human consciousness. As the Cosmic Christ appeared, Teilhard experienced the Divine as a *someone*; he experienced God as *personal*. He could now be in relationship with God and the universe through his entire being.

The mystical circle of the personal is where Teilhard's mysticism becomes "grounded and his synthesis complete."[61] He could see, from this circle, how the complexification of the universe along with its rise in consciousness was moving toward a point of total unity, a convergence that was revealing the emergence of a larger whole in the way he could relate to most as a human.

At this point in Teilhard's journey, the person of Christ came into focus,[62] more profoundly than any human beauty[63] and with a Presence "as immediate and all-embracing as Life."[64] This Presence extended throughout the universe, setting it "ablaze with the fire of divine love, suffused with the elements of a presence that beckons, summons, and embraces" all of humanity.[65] This was the face of the one in whom "all things hold together" (Col 1:17). Teilhard had a devotion to the Sacred Heart of Jesus, traditionally depicted as a red heart, often wrapped in a crown of thorns, bursting with flame and light. This powerful symbol of Christ's total self-offering to the world placed Christ as the vibrant center of the universe.

As Teilhard saw the noosphere reaching its fullness, it was simultaneously revealing the emergence of the Christosphere of unified Christ Consciousness. Earth had evolved to develop what resembled a circulatory system through the biosphere and then a nervous system in the noosphere. Now, in total the human person, evolution had produced a heart.[66] The universe, through the human person, could now love itself.

Teilhard came to understand how the cosmos converging (cosmogenesis) and Christ emerging (Christogenesis) were "two phases of a single evolutionary movement."[67] This synchronicity of Christ and the Omega of the universe released "a light so intense that it transfigured...the very depths of the World."[68] Now, Teilhard could fully embrace his love for the earth. He could comprehend that Christ was at the heart of matter and was alluring him closer, beginning with the Divine Presence in the first circle. Duffy notes that the cosmos, which at first to Teilhard seemed like a "blind and feral immensity, was becoming expressive and personal"[69] by taking on the contours of a body and a face in Christ.[70] Within this fifth mystical circle, Teilhard was able to name this presence as personal.

The emergence of Teilhard's vision of the Cosmic Christ took time to come into focus. At first, he speaks only of encountering "another Thing," a "Presence," "a Soul greater than my own," "a new and super-human Soul," "a personality of another order."[71] These portrayals are impersonal and describe *what* he was encountering. This description transforms and Teilhard eventually names a *who*. The movement from the first Circle of Presence to the last Circle of Person results in this Other, or Godhead, coming to be known as the Cosmic Christ, the Omega Point.[72]

Just as St. Paul declared "Let the same mind be in you that was in Christ Jesus" (Phil 2:5) so "God may be all in all" (1 Cor 15:28), Teilhard proclaims that "when humanity finally transcends itself in Christ, it will inevitably find itself personally immortalized."[73] Teilhard was now aware of how his evolution as a single person played a role within the evolution of the human species. He saw how the evolution of our species was indelibly enmeshed with cosmogenesis and the evolution to Christogenesis.

This sense of belonging set Teilhard's world aflame. He saw Christ's face forming as the world evolved toward this ultimate nexus of convergence and emergence. He was conscious that all the growth, labor, and suffering that he and the rest of the world experienced could be offered for consecration by God's holy fire.[74] The fire drew Teilhard beyond contemplating God's presence to accepting the communion. Teilhard understood that to be one with God, he must be one with the earth. This meant the task of being as conscious as possible of how his life was evolving toward greater relationship with God through Christ Omega.

Thomas King writes that Teilhard did not see destiny as "an impersonal force, but as the action of Christ, the loving Soul of the World."[75] The Cosmic Christ allured Teilhard beyond his individual being to a higher level of awareness, where he could see that it was necessary for him to undertake the duty of cocreating a universe driven to *be more*.

Teilhard affirmed that he was "drawn to follow the road of fire."[76] The road of fire is full of risks and challenges, and inevitably death. However, King observes that "only by an 'annihilation,' passing through a zero point, can one's communion be complete."[77] Teilhard offers himself up "with utter abandon to those fearful forces of dissolution which, I blindly believe, will this day cause my narrow ego to be replaced by your divine presence."[78] He believed that we must pass through total dissolution and then, "as her [his world's] strength fails,...with her he will awaken in the bosom of God."[79] Teilhard was able to love the world. He could love all the growth and the promise of the future, and he could love the impermanence of the past. For Teilhard, nothing was lost. The past was now present in a different state and would, through time and God's grace, be transformed again into something new.

To have a mystical sensibility of the Divine on this level within our lives is, I would argue, natural and ephemeral. To train our "vision" to regularly perceive the Divine is a skill honed through practice. Teilhard's circles provide a guide through which we can deepen our awareness of God's presence around us and within us. More than just taking our awareness of God to new levels, Teilhard's mystical process allows us to further the spiritualization of the universe by *personalizing* the process. The fifth circle empowers an embodiment of the awareness that God is within us and that we are within God.

THE PERSONALIZATION OF THE UNIVERSE

Mystical states of consciousness offer us a sense of intimacy with the Divine and the universe. They are a glimpse into Christ Consciousness, cosmic consciousness, Buddha awareness, or self-actualization. But having a mystical experience does not mean that we have evolved to an advanced level of spiritual and psychological growth. Integration takes lots of hard work, time, and grace.

Teilhard, for example, experienced the Divine Presence initially as an aesthetic mystical encounter. As he progressed through each circle, he encountered the Divine in new ways. He eventually experienced God so personally that he was inspired to live his life in a way where he could be conscious of God in all things.

It took Teilhard time to work through and grow with his mystical experiences. His effort was fruitful as it yielded his experience of the Cosmic Christ, the universal personal. The personal gives context that the universe is in a process of becoming conscious through the human person. Teilhard saw evolution as moving toward forms that express increasing consciousness-complexity in ways that are growing toward advanced self-awareness, thus growing toward *personalization*.

> We often talk of the person as if it represented a (quantitatively) reduced and a (qualitatively) attenuated form of total reality. This is exactly the opposite of what should be understood. The personal is the highest state in which we can grasp the stuff of the universe. In its mysterious atomicity, moreover, something unique and in-transmissible is concentrated, grain by grain.[80]

As consciousness grows and as a personal sense of the universe develops, evolution approaches and crosses a threshold where the process begins to become aware of itself. As we become more integrated psychologically and spiritually, we become more aware of our radical interconnectedness with all life and of our relationship with the Divine. All the while, our consciousness can remain faithful to its presence within *the real*, within the present moment of awareness in the world of matter.

Teilhard was able to articulate his experience of journeying through the evolving cosmic landscape in a way that brought him closer to God, as well as in a way that allowed him to be more deeply engaged in the world. His personal encounter with the Cosmic Christ allowed him an understanding that all human actions contribute to the larger whole of evolution, and that the universe is coming into greater relationship with the Divine via the allure of the Cosmic Christ.

He came to comprehend that his love of the earth was not in opposition to his faith in God. Encountering the earth was the most intimate and personal way that he learned to be in relationship with God. Our relationship with God, like any other, has gifts as well as challenges. This is the road of fire that Teilhard took up to become *more* by offering himself to a reconstitution in and a re-constellation on Christ. In the height of his joy, Teilhard remained diligently aware that the transformation of our being involves sacrifice and the polarity of pain, as well: "For at least three reasons a personalizing evolution is necessarily painful: it is the basis of plurality; it progresses by differentiation; it leads to metamorphosis."[81] A personalizing universe breaks us apart, offers a different perspective of self, and then presents a new and transformed sense of identity. For, if our sense of self is evolving with the ever-dynamic flow of evolution, then we are inevitably moving more integrally into the wholeness, depth, and relationality of God, continually being recreated, and resurrected in a consciousness of our place within the Omega Point.

A universe that becomes more personal allows us to experience the universe in a way that we can feel loved, connected, with a sense of belonging. A personal universe inspires us, like Teilhard, to take up the commissioning of continually cultivating conscious relationship. The mysticism described in Teilhard's five circles is but one perspective of how the human person makes this journey to greater consciousness through union with God. Countless saints, poets, artists, musicians, tradespeople, humanitarians, and a multitude of others from all walks of life have experienced mystical connection with God through ways that are as personal and as unique as the people having the experiences.

Teilhard's copious and meticulous notes make his vision and mysticism more accessible. While his mysticism is layered and complex, it is also systematic and pragmatic. The way he outlines his mystical process to knowing and loving God in deeper ways allows us to venture into our own inner worlds. It calls our awareness to be relational so we can enter more integrally into the world and into matter to *Christify* it: to bring a personal awareness of the sacred.

4

Making Sense of Our Inner World

PSYCHOLOGY WITH A SOUL

Cultures around the world, for ages on end, have recognized the inner world of the human person. We have explored it and created guides through various religions and philosophies. However, it was not until ancient Greece that the study of the inner world, or the soul, was given its namesake in the term *psychology*. The Greek word *psyche* (ψυχή) means "breath, spirit, soul." Thus, psychology translates into not simply a study of the psyche, but rather "the study of the soul." Over time, the modernization of psychological method has shifted. It has moved from analyzing the essence of the human person to strictly focusing on psyche as *mind*. Even more reductively, the mind has been reduced to a purely behavioral mechanism. Certain schools of psychology, however, have maintained that the psyche is more than one's mental perception of and interaction with the world, and is greater than the outcome of an individual's behavioral tendencies.

The foundation of modern psychology is traced back to the philosopher William James (1842–1910). James noted that there are several elements that make up the human psyche—what he refers to as the "self." According to James, there is the material self, the social self, the spiritual self, and the pure ego (Latin for *I*, or one's sense of self).[1] Sigmund Freud (1856–1939), the Austrian neurologist and founder of modern psychoanalysis, divided the psyche into three parts: id, ego, and superego. The id operates on the "pleasure principle" and is the root of basic impulses and drives, seeking immediate gratification. The superego is the unbiased moral component of the psyche. Between these two poles is the ego. According to Freud, the ego is like a charioteer who is tasked with providing direction for the two horses (id and superego) at either side.[2]

Swiss psychiatrist and psychoanalyst Carl Gustav Jung (1875–1961) viewed human consciousness in a larger context. Jung saw the psyche as part of a larger process within nature. The human psyche was the result of "a cosmos laboring through timeless aeons to give birth to this rare quality that we call consciousness."[3] Jung was mentored for some time by Freud and was initially seen to be his successor, but the two eventually had a professional disagreement and Jung broke off to form his own method of psychoanalysis.

Unlike Freud, Jung did not view the unconscious mind as a mere appendage to the conscious mind. Jungian therapist Robert Johnson writes how, for Jung, "the unconscious is the Original Mind of humankind, the primal matrix out of which our species has evolved a conscious mind and then developed it over millennia to the extent and the refinement that it has today."[4] Therefore, Jung's model is much more expansive and dynamic in that it recognizes the psyche as a product of billions of years of evolution.

Thus, the ego is not simply a navigator being propelled by forces of impulse and moral duty. Instead, it is our sense of identity (*I*) that is like a ship navigating its way from sea to harbor with the guidance of a lighthouse. Jung's model of the psyche is made up of Freud's three components of id, ego, and superego. He also includes dynamics such as the *persona*, the *shadow*, *archetypes*, *anima* and *animus*, and the *Self*. His model of psychic growth is directed toward wholeness and emphasizes the importance of the individual psyche.[5] In this way, Jung's approach to psychology is much more akin to the notion of the psyche as *soul*, as it was originally defined by the Greeks.

Furthermore, Jung's thought includes the role of the supernatural within the process of psychological growth. His doctoral dissertation was titled *On the Psychology and Pathology of So-Called Occult Phenomena*. Later in his career he studied the psychological implications of alchemy—the esoteric practice of transmuting base metals into precious metals and precursor to chemistry. Jung even took his theory of *synchronicity*, or meaningful coincidences, and began working with theoretical physicist and pioneer of quantum physics Wolfgang Pauli in attempt to understand the link between subjective consciousness and the objective world. The two men were fascinated with how, within our subjective consciousness and sometimes even within experiences of collective consciousness, there appears a meaningful correlation between our inner world and the outer world.

According to psychoanalyst and scholar Anthony Stevens, Jung understood how the "psyche of Nature slowly made itself conscious," believing that "God and all of creation labored through time to bring conscious awareness into the universe."[6] Religion, for Jung, was a crucial part of the whole-making process for the individual and the world. While the relevance of religion might be seen as empirically subjective, its function is rather pragmatic. Freud's view of religion had reduced to purely psychoanalytic scrutiny. Meanwhile, Jung's exposure to global cultures and his contact with the collective unconscious framed religion as a way that the human psyche attempts to connect with a larger dimension of existence. This idea became central to Jung's model psychic growth and his method of analysis. Roles of saviors, messiahs, and heroes within cultural and religious contexts intrigued Jung. He recognized each of these individuals' trials and triumphs as indicative of the psyche's natural inclination toward transcendence of itself through finding a more altruistic purpose within the world.

This laborious process of psychological growth in Jungian lexicon is called *individuation*, or the lifelong process of becoming the "complete human beings we were born to be."[7] Individuation is a process by which we come into our own authentic being, "allowing our conscious personalities to develop until they include all the basic elements inherent in each of us at the preconscious level."[8] Jung chose the term *individuation* because it captures the essence of the process—actualizing a person's unique psychic *individuality*. Individuation allows us the ability to engage more fully with the world. Jungian individuation mirrors Teilhard's notion of creative union, wherein "everything...is formed by successive unifications of the multiple."[9] For, once we feel more whole and unified within ourselves, it is natural also to seek the countless ways that we resemble our fellow human beings through the "the values, interests, and essentially human qualities that bind us together in the human tribe."[10] Individuation is our life's work, achieved by the unique way we combine and integrate the energy systems and material of our psyche.

TEILHARD AND JUNG

Both Teilhard and Jung lived during the dawn of the twentieth century and hold similar ideas regarding consciousness as the driving force behind evolution. However, the two men never met in person, nor exchanged any sort of correspondence. Any evidence of their knowledge of one another is anecdotal. What proof does exist neither confirms nor denies whether they influenced each other. Thomas King remarks that Teilhard's familiarity with Jung is "best seen in the way he spells Jung as 'Young' or 'Yung.'"[11] However, in a personal letter to a friend, Teilhard recommends Jung's article, "Does the World Stand on the Verge of a Spiritual Rebirth?" In the letter, Teilhard notes that Jung's ideas, in their essence, are "curiously similar to [his]."[12] It is only from a comment by Jung's friend, Miguel Serrano, that it is known that the Swiss psychotherapist was aware of the Jesuit. Serrano visited Jung shortly before his death in 1961 and tells of walking into Jung's room, spotting *The Human Phenomenon* on the table next to Jung's chair. Serrano asked if he had read the book. Jung simply replied, "It is a great book."[13]

Without using the term *individuation*, Teilhard affirms that "union differentiates."[14] The interaction and union of elements reveal the emergence of something new with greater potential. The coming together of different elements to form something more can be found everywhere in creation. Hydrogen and oxygen atoms come together to form water molecules; a sperm and an egg unite to yield a zygote. Differentiation demonstrates how complexity occurs at all levels, a result of matter's propensity to develop intimate relationships.[15] This tendency in nature to become more complex and more conscious allows for us to break through boundaries into new realms of evolutionary awareness.

Teilhard examines creative union as a process in both the psyche and in the world. Jung almost exclusively focuses on the internal, psychic element. He observes that when our conscious mind begins to dialogue with the unconscious, we begin to evolve through distinct stages in our psychological growth. We must evolve through stages of darkness and light along with confrontations with our rejected or unknown personalities as we individuate. Like Teilhard's journey into the heart of matter, diving into the unconscious should be taken with great caution, as it holds the incomprehensible power to alter our worldview and our being.

With the help of a psychoanalyst or perhaps even with assistance from healthy cultural and religious immersion and practices, we can integrate the different components of the unconscious into our conscious mind. This integration emerges as an awareness of the wholeness of our being through our relationship with the many smaller parts that compose it. As a result, a healthy psyche can draw energy from these forces when it is appropriate. It is not driven by the unconscious forces having "a mind of their own." We are able to flourish with authenticity while serving the larger whole.

THE UNCONSCIOUS

Jung views consciousness as an energy emanating from evolution's flow toward higher states of being. He recognizes the different levels of consciousness that exist throughout nature, and how human consciousness is unique given its capacity for self-reflection. Unconscious drives, according to Freud, stem from the repression of sexuality and anger. Jung postures, however, that the unconscious has two distinct identities. The first is its personal identity, or the unconscious contents exclusive to individual persons: the personal unconscious. The second is the *collective unconscious*, a term coined by Jung that accounts for the unconscious contents inherited by all human beings, extending back through the entire history of the species.

The personal unconscious is made up of elements from our human experience. We had been conscious of this material, but it slipped out of consciousness and into our personal unconscious because it was forgotten or repressed. The contents of the personal unconscious might include anything from the time spent in our mother's womb, to childhood experiences, to more recent events. It is necessary that we have a healthy connection with our personal unconscious and that we do the work of integrating its material as we grow.

Jung's personal experiences and observations of global cultures led him to the conclusion that there was an even larger unconscious network that consciousness was emanating from. The personal unconscious could not be the sum of all consciousness. He arrived at the idea of how the collective unconscious is a larger system of consciousness that predates the individual's personal unconscious. This is the deepest level of our psyche, housing the ancestral psychic material of our species. The collective unconscious contains experience so ancient that it transcends language. It is often experienced by way of symbols, feelings, and imagery that we begin to identify in our waking life or, most commonly, in our dreams.

The collective unconscious is found to be the "creative source of all that evolves into the conscious mind and in the total personality of each individual."[16] It is the raw material from which our conscious minds develop, mature, and expand. In Teilhardian fashion, Jung also affirms that "each person is the microcosm through which the universal process of consciousness actualizes itself."[17] Thus, Jung views consciousness as an organ of reality, so to speak, that is evolving in its importance within nature. As a phenomenon of self-awareness, the human person is how the universe is becoming aware of itself. Just as every aspect of nature has its place within a larger system or state of equilibrium, the development of the human person through the expression of its personality (that is to say, its consciousness) is integral to the functioning of the world.

THE EGO

As we individuate, our psyche passes through the stages of centration, decentration, and super-centration. The ego demonstrates centration, where we establish our individual, separate self. The ego's job is to integrate the contents of the unconscious into our conscious personality. The ego exists as a matter of survival. Thus, many egocentric thoughts and actions are often not as selfishly centered as we might think. Instead, egoic individuals are often acting out of fear or the need to *survive*. The ego, however, is also what allows us to develop a firm and confident disposition, which we can offer in service of others as opposed to solely catering to our own needs. Contemporary spiritual teacher Ram Dass credits Swami Vivekananda with saying that "the ego is a lousy master but a wonderful servant."[18]

Therefore, it is not always fair to view a strong ego as a bad thing. In fact, notable figures such as Jesus of Nazareth, Martin Luther King Jr., and Mother Theresa possessed incredibly robust egos. The caveat is that we allow our egos to be in service of a higher reality, our "Higher Self."[19] An *egocentric* individual, on the other hand, sees themselves as the center of reality. Legere refers to the ego as a "planet of the soul" that has "its own orbit" around the Higher Self.[20] It is a matter of the planet shifting back into orbit, allowing the ego to find its place. Legere points out how the ego is sometimes pitted as the enemy of spiritual growth. Instead, the ego is a prerequisite for it.[21] The adversary of spiritual growth is not the ego—as it often is displayed in popular interpretations of spiritual growth—but rather what Legere calls a "me" consciousness:

> Note that, in English, the word "me" is in the lower case, unlike the word "I." When we are speaking from the vantage point of our "me" state of consciousness, we are on

> an entirely different frequency. "Me"-thinking is fear-based and thinks in terms of separateness. This is the "unworthy" part of us that is in "sin" ("missing the mark" in Greek); this is the part of us that contributes to the disorder in our world.[22]

Fortunately, our ego has options when it comes to facing the unknown depths of the unconscious, as well as the unpredictability of dealing with indefinite variables present in the physical world. Our ego can grow to be a healthy expression of our *personality*—"a combination of that within us which is innate (genes, temperament, and type) along with our character (the person that we choose to become)."[23] The word "personality" comes from *persona*, Latin for mask. According to Jung, "The persona is a complicated system of relations between individual consciousness and society, fittingly enough a kind of mask, designed on the one hand to make a definite impression upon others, and, on the other, to conceal the true nature of the individual."[24]

It is common for us to wear masks at different times throughout our lives. It is natural for different parts of our personality to be amplified or subdued as we function in different roles. This is not unhealthy, if we can take off the mask when appropriate. The point of these masks is that we use them functionally and recognize they are meant to be optional and interchangeable. It has often been misunderstood that our egos and personas are negative things. Instead, it is overidentification with our egos and misuse (and even abuse) of our personas that lead our psychic development to balk and even to potentially develop into a neurosis or, at worst, a psychosis.

Our ego provides us with a sense of our individual identity (centration). Psychological growth calls us to move beyond the ego (decentration) through interaction with others, the world, and our unconscious. The ego maintains a tension between our conscious attitude and the content of the unconscious. This tension is necessary for our psychological growth. As the ego sustains a healthy pressure imposed by the conscious and unconscious attitudes, a fuller image of our personality begins to emerge.

THE UNION OF OPPOSITES AND THE TRANSCENDENT FUNCTION

We are neurologically wired for "binary opposition." According to Jeffrey Miller, binary opposition is a natural psychic "tendency to separate reality into pairs of opposites pervasive in the human experience."[25] This tendency presents itself as a tension of dualities significant to the human endeavor: life/death, light/dark, spirit/matter, inner/outer, good/bad, love/hate, and so on. Neurologically, there is evidence that shows how "neurons, the cells that make up the brain, are essentially on/off switches; they are either stimulated enough by the electric charge coming across the synapse from the neighboring neuron to fire a signal to the next neuron or they are not."[26]

There is also speculation that the physiological basis for binary opposition might be found in the two-hemisphere structure of the brain. The left brain performs logical, reasoning functions and tends to focus more on the ego/me/self-perceptions. The right hemisphere processes things "in an analogical or metaphorical style"[27] and "sees parts as having meaning only within a context."[28] The right half creates the experience of "otherness" in terms of an opposition from oneself. In the right brain, parts only have meaning within a context. Therefore, communication between hemispheres is crucial for healthy psychological functionality. The logic of the left helps to validate the context of relationships perceived by the right, and the right allows the left to see the value of the whole made up of many intentionally interconnected and interdependent parts.

Jung's method examines how the human person derives meaning from duality, using it as a point for growth and integration. Jung saw this law of psychic opposition as similar to the first law of thermodynamics: All energy is a function of two opposing forces.[29] Psychologically, this is the tension between the conscious ego and unconscious mind. Our task to unite these opposites is a cosmic endeavor, where we are the vessel through which nature continues to carry out its mission of forming united wholes from separate parts.

Jung incorporates the philosophical concept of the *unio oppositorum*, or the union of opposites. The union of opposites is when we approach a traditionally viewed duality as a union, or from a nondual perspective. Psychologically, our ego stands at the crux of this merger, where it is tasked with maintaining the tension between our unconscious mind and our conscious mind (the opposites, in this case) so that the Self (the larger, nondual identity) can emerge from the tension between the ego and the unconscious. Jung named the emergence that occurs from this tension the Transcendent Function.

The Transcendent Function arises "from the union of the conscious and unconscious contents" to produce a wholly new perspective.[30] The word *transcendent* marks the transition from one attitude to another. At first, these attitudes are in tension with one another. "The confrontation of the two positions generates a tension charged with energy and creates a living, third thing...a movement out of the suspension between opposites, a living birth that leads to a new level of being, a new situation."[31] This "living thing" for Jung is a new state of consciousness that arises from the tension, and eventually integration, of the conscious ego and unconscious mind. It is a more authentic expression of our personality, of our soul. *Soul*, for Jung, implies a perspective rather than a substance.[32]

This new and living thing that emerges from the tension held between opposites is real and embodied through our personality.

The transcendent function emerges from our ego's mediation of the contents of our unconscious into consciousness. It is like a bridge between the objectivity of our unconscious and the subjectivity of our conscious ego. The Transcendent Function marks the super-centering of our ego on the Self. The ego realigns on the Center. But since the ego achieves this position through interaction with the unconscious, the ego maintains its identity without the previously perceived need to retain control. Our ego preserves our identity, which is now more authentic through our conscious connection to a larger reality. Consequentially, we realize we are part of a larger universe.[33] As the ego super-centers on the Self through the Transcendent Function, the ego claims something that is within itself, but not itself. The higher state of consciousness found within the Self allows us to become aware of our unique and authentic identity within the larger whole.

THE SELF

The goal of individuation is integration of the Self. The Self represents our psyche *as a whole*. It is the union of our conscious and unconscious minds. We can also say that the Self is the Transcendent Function. It can only be revealed as we hold the tension within us between our awareness and everything beyond it.

The Self, according to Marie-Louise von Franz, "is not entirely contained in our conscious experience of time (in our space-time dimension), and is also simultaneously omnipresent."[34] In fact, the Self "appears frequently in a form that hints at a special omnipresence; that is, it manifests itself as a gigantic, symbolic human being who embraces and contains the whole cosmos."[35] Individuation is a life-long process; thus, the Self is our life's great work, our own magnum opus.

In this regard, the Self is teleological, or with a purpose. In the Self, we are drawn to recognize our whole nature. The Self is the space where the opposites are held in union. We are conscious of our good qualities, as well as the less-than-desirable aspects of our personality. The Self is not our perfection, and it is not meant to be. In the way that Jesus calls to us to *whole*, the Self draws us to be *complete* human beings.

The awareness we experience when we are in conscious relationship with the Self is the very energy of evolution rising up inside of us. The rise in consciousness initiated by the Self is complemented by further complexification of the neurons in our brain. Our new consciousness in the Self results in the emergence of new neural pathways through which we can perceive and engage the world; our psychological growth has a very real impact on our evolution as a species.

Jung looks at the psyche as a living organism within the human being. This organism is seeking its fulfillment in a goal:

> Life is an energy-process. Like every energy-process, it is in principle irreversible and is therefore directed towards a goal. That goal is a state of rest. In the long run everything that happens is, as it were, no more than the initial disturbance of a perpetual state of rest which forever attempts to re-establish itself. Life is teleology *par excellence*; it is the intrinsic striving towards a goal, and the living organism is a system of directed aims which seek to fulfill themselves.[36]

Without a doubt, the ways in which humanity has expressed this supposedly innate drive for a goal have been questionable at times. The pursuit of the goal Jung speaks of has sometimes historically taken paths of *self*-interest (*ego*-interest), as opposed to *Self*-interest. Humanity has selfishly turned-in on itself, and it has even turned against itself in hate. But it has also risen above with shining models of selfless love, compassion, and justice. There are countless examples of people who have viewed their lives as being part of a larger effort. In striving to be a contributing unit in the functioning and existence of the overall human organism, these people show us how to put service of Self above ourselves, or above our egos.

The Self integrates the good as well as the bad, so that we can become conscious of the whole. Everything known about life, from the nearness of biology, to the far reaches of astronomy, demonstrates that the evolutionary climb is a journey of some duration and distance. Evolution reaches toward a goal of wholeness. The journey to wholeness is filled with the flux of novelty and entropy. The work of individuation is the work of evolution.

THE CHRIST ARCHETYPE

Jung resists making metaphysical claims about the psyche and his psychoanalytic method. Yet, in some cases, he cannot help but use religious language when describing certain dynamics and elements of psychological growth. Jung describes the collective unconscious as the "whole spiritual heritage of [hu]mankind's evolution, born anew in the brain structure of every individual."[37] In his interpretation of the unconscious and its purpose within the life of the human person and evolution, he writes:

> The collective unconscious—so far as we can say anything about it at all—appears to consist of mythological motifs or primordial images, for which reason the myths of all nations are its real exponents. In fact, the whole of mythology could be taken as a sort of projection of the

> collective unconscious....We can therefore study the collective unconscious in two ways, either in mythology or in the analysis of the individual.[38]

Within the collective unconscious there are universal psychological structures and energy systems that we all have in common. Jung calls these primordial patterns *archetypes*. Archetypes are present within all of us and aggregate within an infinite number of combinations, forming our unique personalities and our distinct psychological structures. The ways in which these universal energies combine *within* each of us and are consciously expressed *through* each of us are ultimately a collective expression of the unconscious as a now conscious entity.

The Self, while a "real" thing, can also be seen as an archetype of totality. Jung is moved to declare that "Christ exemplifies the archetype of the Self."[39] He understands Christ, historically, as marking the shift from the human psyche projecting its sense of spiritual connectedness via organized religions and onto the embodiment of this archetype. Jesus refers to his identification as the central source of psychic development in phrases such as "I am the vine, you are the branches" (John 15:5). Christ holds the tension in the union of opposites in his identification as "I am Alpha and Omega" (Rev 1:8). There is a sense of completion and totality in not only the figure of Christ as an archetype independent of the psyche, but also as a fulfillment of the total psyche.

Jung writes, "He is the vine, and those that hang on him are the branches. His body is to be eaten, and his blood wine to be drunk; he is also the mystical body formed by the congregation."[40] Christ is the Good Shepherd, he is the leader and the center of the flock. In iconography, Christ is often at the center surrounded by the quaternity of the evangelists along with the angels and saints. Jung understands this imagery as symbolizing the integration of the kings and prophets of the Old Testament, concentrated and fulfilled in the complete person of Christ.

On another level, Jung sees the symbolism of the "four" and the "twelve" as indicators of wholeness. Christ is surrounded by the four evangelists and the twelve disciples. The fourfold structure of the cross is even the means through which Jesus of Nazareth enters into the fullness of the human experience in death, emerging as the risen Christ. The number four can be seen as symbolizing stability and rootedness in the world. There are four classical elements, four seasons, four directions, four corners of the earth. The number twelve symbolizes cosmic order as shown through the twelve months of the year, the twelve signs of the zodiac, the twelve disciples, the twelve tribes of Israel, the twelve pearled gates of Jerusalem, and the crown of twelve stars in Revelation.

Christ embodies all mythological truths—both from within Christianity and outside of it—about both the human and the cosmos in conscious union. According to Jung, "Christ adumbrates an archetype that expresses itself in essentially the same symbolism and also occurs in individual dreams or in fantasy-like projections upon living people (transference phenomena, hero worship, etc.)."[41] The archetype of Christ is an integrated expression of the idea of "an overpowering, all-embracing, complete or perfect being, represented by either a man of heroic proportions, or by an animal with magical attributes, or by a magical vessel or some other geometrically, by a mandala."[42] Truth can be found in many places and in many forms. Yet it is in Christ that we are affirmed of *who* is true. Furthermore, we can discover truth within ourselves.

The truth of Christ's being, in that sense, is also problematic for Jung looking at Christ as the archetype of the total person. Christ, born without sin and the influence of evil, is lacking that component of the human experience, that sense of incompleteness and imperfection. However, what is unique in this case is that the fullness of the Christ emerges after the person of Jesus of Nazareth, who bears the archetype, experiences the totality of the human experience by being put to death at the hands of the collective.[43] In order for us to experience the fullness of the Christ archetype, we must also enter with our ego into the unconscious to emerge with a conscious relationship with the Self. In a way, the Christ archetype calls us all to participate within the whole. To fully embody itself as an archetypal reality, or, a real and physical center through which the Divine is consciously present within the world and our lived experience, we must all strive to become the complete humans we are called to be.

5

Understanding Teilhard's Integration

THE FOUR PSYCHIC FUNCTIONS

Carl Jung's work is an invaluable guide for exploring our psychological growth. As he studied global cultures, he was exposed to their mythologies. Jung saw how the motifs in mythology were reflective of various stages of psychological growth.

The two guiding myths through Teilhard's life were evolution and Christ. He could not disconnect his faith in the world and his love of God. So, he used them, together, to participate more fully in the world and grow closer to God. By allowing himself to delve into the "gray area" between the supposed duality between matter and spirit, Teilhard allowed himself access to his inner world. He did not do his inner work while in the quiet cell of a monastery with its predictable rhythm of life. Teilhard went deep within himself on the European front of World War I, in the deserts of China, and in the electric energy of New York City. His immersion in the world and with people from all walks of life demanded that he develop an integrated awareness. If he was to thrive, let alone survive, he had to have a healthy sense of self and a balanced awareness of how he could connect to others and the world.

This was a process for Teilhard. In the section to follow, we will join Teilhard on his inner journey as we are guided by a Jungian commentary of Teilhard's process. To fully experience God, Teilhard had to fully experience matter. As a result, he had to fully experience himself and all his spiritual depth. In the most practical sense, this means that Teilhard needed to venture into his unconscious mind to claim the parts of himself that had not yet been discovered.

While our inner world contains psychic energies and archetypes that guide us along our development, Jung identifies four basic functions of the psyche. These functions need to be in a proper state of balance to appropriately integrate the other contents of the unconscious into our conscious personality.

The four basic functions, according to Jung, are *thinking, feeling, sensing,* and *intuiting*. *Thinking* pertains to logical analysis. *Feeling* is our access to sentiment and emotion. *Sensing* interprets physical and sensual data. *Intuiting* is an instinctual knowing, usually of dynamics unseen or unverifiable.

Thinking and feeling have to do with arriving at conclusions; sensation and intuition are for perception, or the gathering of information.[1] Generally, people are dominant in some of these functions, while other functions are neglected. Neglected functions fall into the unconscious, from where they must be retrieved during the individuation process. When we reclaim neglected functions, we restore greater balance to our psyche.

Let us look at Jesus as an example. Jesus's psychological profile exemplifies a balanced and integrated psyche. When Jesus is faced with situations that call for quick logical analysis and objective thought, such as in his intellectual bouts with the Pharisees, his astute and intelligent responses are a sign that he is integrated as a thinking person.[2] John Sanford notes the many instances where Jesus is moved with compassion for others, showing "the great value that he places on individual life," a telltale characteristic of the feeling function.[3]

Jesus's teachings and parables, which used common and worldly examples, showcase a well-developed sensation function. Raised as a carpenter, Jesus had an intimate relationship with matter and the natural world. His "immediate contact with the inner world, his use of images, and his sensing of realities not visible to the senses but known to the inner vision" reveal a keen intuitive function. His intuitive function is also obvious in his insight into human souls.[4] He is a model for wholeness and psychological integration.

Balancing the components of the psyche to allow our authentic personality to express itself is no small task. In fact, it is a cosmically important task, for order within the human person is essential for cosmic order. Super-centration of oneself (ego) upon the Self, to use Legere's earlier analogy, is like a planet in its correct orbit around the axis point of the Self, the Higher Center upon which reality rests.

TEILHARD'S DESCENT INTO THE UNCONSCIOUS AS AN *INTUITIVE* TYPE

We now return to Teilhard's rich personal accounts of his encounters with the Divine. These mystical vignettes provide insight into the psychological processes unfolding within Teilhard as he grows toward greater wholeness. Teilhard's documentation is a Jungian's dream. It is poetic and full of imagery, yet sharply empirical and analogical as Teilhard does his best to describe his inner world.

In Thomas King's *Jung's Four and Some Philosophers: A Paradigm for Philosophy*, he demonstrates the Jungian dynamics at work in Teilhard's life and thought. In King's analysis,

Teilhard is an intuitive type. Teilhard's intuitive function is highlighted in his seeking a "scientific recasting of knowing: intuition replacing deduction"[5] and a metaphysics based on "intuitive induction."[6] King uses Teilhard's 1916 essay "Cosmic Life" to highlight the dominance of Teilhard's intuitive function, as well as identifying the sensation function that Teilhard needed to integrate.

"Cosmic Life" is Teilhard's first written account of his mystical vision of the cosmos awakening. The essay is divided into two subsections titled "La Vision" and "La Sensation." King notes how "La Vision" "appeals to [the] contemporary scientific picture wherein...all things share a common origin and a common growth; all things are *seen* as elements of the total development of the cosmos."[7] "La Sensation," on the other hand, is an expression of Teilhard's recognition that "it is not enough to observe [*regarder*] from the outside the cosmic currents taking shape...we must be able to feel [*sentir*] them."[8] Thus, while "La Vision" tells of Teilhard's external vision regarding the journey of the cosmos, "La Sensation" is his personal account of his path inward to seek how he might evolve, in sync with the universe. King notes that, in "La Sensation," "[Teilhard's] imagery tells of a personal descent into the unconscious."[9] Teilhard's description of his voyage into the depths of his psyche overflows with Jungian themes that represent encountering the unconscious as a "descent" into a body of water, a basement, a cave, or darkness:

> And I allowed my consciousness to sweep back to the farthest limit of my body, to ascertain whether I might not extend outside myself. I stepped down into the most hidden depths of my being, lamp in hand and ears alert, to discover whether, in the deepest recesses of the blackness within me, I might not see the glint of the waters of the current that flows on, whether I might not hear

> the murmur of their mysterious waters that rise from the uttermost depths and will burst forth, no man knows where. With terror and intoxicating emotion, I realized that my own poor trifling existence was one with the immensity of all that is and all that is still in process of becoming. I can feel it: matter, which I thought was most my own, eludes and escapes me.[10]

As Teilhard's conscious awareness was confronted by the unconscious, he was forced to let go of his attachments to what he held true about himself and his understanding of reality. This forceful encounter with his unconscious became an opportunity for Teilhard to reclaim his sensing function. As his inferior function, Teilhard's sensing function was not within his conscious field of awareness. Therefore, when he plunged into his unconscious, he was confronted with the reality that the matter making own being was not truly his own. King sees Teilhard as being "surrounded by a mass of unconscious forces that escape his control."[11] Teilhard became aware that "his life was not his own, for his inmost soul was one with the universe"[12] as he underwent a decentration and then a supercentration of his being.

NAVIGATING THE UNCONSCIOUS

Teilhard penned "Cosmic Life" while serving as a stretcher bearer in the French army during World War I. The trauma of war filled Teilhard with what Freud terms "oceanic feelings" as he felt his consciousness slip away, leaving him "more or less dissolved into a bliss-giving repose."[13] Teilhard was led to this feeling of reprieve by a "feminine" presence, which Jung refers to as *anima*. Teilhard's words describe the relational nature of this feminine energy, as he identifies "the rich, the mother, the divine" as the "fertile, generatrix, the Terra Mater."[14] Jung identified the anima as the soul guide of the man. The anima is the force capable of leading a man to his authentic Self. Thus, Teilhard was allured by the anima deeper into matter in his continued search for union with God.

Teilhard followed the call of the feminine and was led to the experience of feeling one with the universe. However, Teilhard found his awareness was falling back to a prehistoric point in time, where he perceived matter as a disjointed nothingness. He felt as if he was present within the elementary stages of the universe, long before the evolution of the human person. He discovered himself surrounded by matter that was less complex and, therefore, "of primordial consciousness," where he "finds the light of life was dimmed."[15] At first, he found this was a welcome pause from the horrors of war. Yet, when he realized that he was moving counter to evolution, he saw that he was drifting away from the permanence he was seeking at the heart of matter.

While submersed within the "little-known depths" of the unconsciousness, Teilhard experienced what he called "a diminution of personality."[16] In the Jungian sense, this "diminution of personality" translates as the reduction of ego identity via a descent into the unconscious.[17] At this point in his journey, Teilhard stopped descending any further. He attributed his "faith in life"[18] with saving him from drifting too deeply into disintegration. He halted his descent into the primordial universe, reversed direction, and then coordinated his rise with the ascent of evolution: "We must travel with our backs to matter and not try to return to it and be absorbed into it.... Now, like a diver who regains control and masters his inertia, I must make a vigorous effort, reverse my course and ascend again to the higher levels."[19]

Teilhard's ascent is not a rejection of matter. Instead, King asserts that Teilhard's experience taught him that "one first must make a descent into matter (the unconscious), and then reverse direction and ascend."[20] By descending into matter (the unconscious), he encountered the perspective (energies and archetypes) that allowed him to experience wholeness in a way that he had not before (encountering his sensing function integrated with his other functions). Having had this experience, Teilhard witnessed a perspective—that is, a level of consciousness—where he came to communion with God through union with the earth.

"God is identified as the heavenly Word, Light, and consciousness," writes King, "but the way to attain communion with God is indirect: it begins with descent into earthly silence, darkness, and unconsciousness."[21] Therefore, Teilhard's balancing of his intuitive function was part of a "process which involves distress, disintegration, loss, and sorrow."[22] It moved him to a feeling of "religious horror"[23] as he felt his conscious mind falling back into matter, grasping at air when trying to cling to the very matter that he took for granted as being his own, his physical manifestation in the world. Yet, in the decentering of his ego, a new consciousness emerged. Teilhard experienced matter with a degree of purity through his sensing function. Subsequently, he accessed an awareness of his connectedness to the Divine in a way that had transcended all other such experiences or feelings of relationship. Having encountered God in this way, Teilhard was now aware of the importance of this understanding as he ascended to consciousness.

ASCENDING TO CONSCIOUSNESS IN THE PERSONAL

Teilhard's ascent to consciousness demonstrates how discovering and integrating the inferior function is vital in coming to psychological wholeness. In Teilhard's personal case, he declares that "the mystical effort to *see* must give way to the effort to *feel* [*sentir*] and to surrender."[24] He acknowledges this integration of his sensing function. The newly integrated function is a pathway to the Self in such a way that Jung often spoke of retrieving the missing function by quoting the Scriptures: "The stone the builders rejected has become the cornerstone."[25] Experiencing God through his sensing function, Teilhard tells of how the "Godhead gradually assumes, in our sentient faculty [*notre faculté de sentir*] the higher Reality it possesses in the nature of things."[26]

In "Cosmic Life," Teilhard's description of his communion with the Divine (Christ, the Self, etc.) is rather brief. Other than referring to the "Godhead"[27] and recognizing that "all things were moving towards the Child born of Woman,"[28] Teilhard's account of union with the All is sparse. In "The Mystical Milieu," however, Teilhard describes his process of coming to communion with the Divine in a much more elaborate and eloquent fashion. "The Mystical Milieu" was written a year after "Cosmic Life" and illustrates how, after Teilhard's initial mystical encounter described in his first essay, he was able to incorporate the content of that experience. This integration allowed him to arrive at a more coherent, refined, and authentic way of being in union with God.

"The Mystical Milieu" recounts a similar event in which Teilhard descends into his unconscious and has an experience with his sensing function, reverses, and ascends to consciousness. King writes that Teilhard's second essay provides "a detailed account of the final Christ, the mysterious and very personal Focus that resembles what Jung associates with the Christ of the mystics and called the Transcendent Function or the Self."[29] The essay serves as an excellent tool for understanding how the psychic process works toward wholeness. Beginning with his ego consciousness, Teilhard is "at one point, in a person: my own person." He is then overtaken by sensations of sound, light, and color and is drawn out of himself "into an even richer and more spiritual rhythm that was imperceptible and endlessly becoming the measure of all growth and all beauty."[30] Having moved beyond his ego consciousness, Teilhard demonstrates the integration of his sensing function as he is now able to encounter God everywhere in the world: "Under this single tangible stuff, Lord, you make yourself manifest to us and fill us with rapture."[31] God is in *the real*: in the body and in the world.

With this new consciousness of the Divine as his boon, Teilhard stops his descent, once again, and ascends from the unconscious to consciousness. His rise in this essay describes how his awareness becomes super-centered on a new and higher center: "I recognized that it was all coming to a center on a single point, on a Person: your Person: Jesus!"[32] What Teilhard once described ambiguously as "another Thing," and "a Presence and super-human Soul,"[33] is now given a more personal tone. The "unknown" and the "Godhead" had become the Self, the super-Personal.[34] The super-Personal is not nebulous. It has a face, a name, a body, and a heart. And it lives within us!

The Divine had been present within the world of matter all along, Teilhard had not known how to apply himself in the appropriate ways to arrive at such an encounter and understanding. It took the stresses of war to capsize Teilhard's ego, so to speak, so that he could dive into the unknown waters of the unconscious and retrieve the buried treasure of consciousness. In his consciousness becoming super-centered, he could now see that the amorphous Divine that he sought in the universe was so real that he could have a relationship with God in a way that was most personal. Teilhard found that we can "worship in ourselves something is 'us.' God with us!"[35] Through recovering his inferior function, Teilhard accessed an awareness of God within himself.

THE OMEGA POINT AND THE JUNGIAN QUATERNITY

The psychological implications of Teilhard's mysticism, from a Jungian perspective, are not only in the visionary experiences themselves. Teilhard's larger vision also contains powerful symbolism. Ultimately, Teilhard's awareness of his union with God allowed him a sense of duty and purpose in evolution. He came to see how every human life is interconnected with cosmic life, and that all life was converging to reveal an even greater identity within the universe: the emergent Christ Omega. The imagery of the Omega Point is pregnant with Jungian tones that correlate with the idea of the Self.

King explains Jung's understanding of the Self as "a mysterious Other, as ourselves, and more than ourselves."[36] Developing an awareness of the Self results from having worked through the contents of the unconscious to retrieve an awareness that was previously inaccessible. Thus, the greater identity and awareness that we encounter in the Self is, in part, transcendent. Jung often saw this process as a matter of "three-becoming-four," where our retrieval of the rejected function yields the missing cornerstone of consciousness. In Jung's study of cultures and peoples from around the world, he recognized one of the foremost universal motifs to be the symbolism of the number four as representing balance and stability.

Teilhard assigned the Omega Point four attributes: autonomy, actuality, irreversibility, and transcendence. Thus, King writes how "Omega could be said to be three parts evolutionary process (transience) and one-part transcendent God, 3-becomes-4."[37] The first three attributes—autonomy, actuality, and irreversibility—come by way of cosmic evolution. The fourth, transcendence, is distinguished from the other three in a way that reconciles the three in their convergence with the fourth to form a whole. This new whole can be considered the Christic. The reality that emerges from this convergence is the Self, the Cosmic Christ Omega.

"Omega obviously resembles what Jung called the Self," writes King, as it "unites four qualities."[38] Teilhard recognized Omega as the "higher pole of evolution" where "radii meet."[39] King writes that "the evolutionary process itself involves much transience; but the term of the process is the transcendent God. God is entering the process of evolution; by doing so the transcendent God gives the transient process what the process does not have, stability."[40] The stability provided by the fourth is present within the psyche, but it is not actualized until, like Teilhard, we descend into our unconscious to become conscious of the missing function.

In accessing his sensing function and encountering the Divine in a way that was so personal, Teilhard came to a tangible awareness of the purpose and meaning in his human life in the scope of evolution. Teilhard felt that the convergence of humanity was catalyzing the emergence of a higher consciousness in Omega. He writes of how the human person constitutes a "knot whose strands have been for all time converging from the four corners of space."[41] The God whom Teilhard found in himself was the God whom he encountered in the world. By accessing the God in himself, Teilhard's consciousness expanded so that his being became super-centered on Omega, the center of all relationship. Therefore, Teilhard's thought resounds with a call for us, as a collective human organism, to do the same. The final Omega, according to Teilhard, is evolution's "supreme pole of interiorization," a "transcendent focus" that is "born of involution."[42] *Involution* refers the expansion of our inner world, while evolution is the outward growth of the universe.

Jung's inclusion of the visionary experience within his method of psychoanalysis is invaluable. It provides a pathway for understanding our inner experience. Even more importantly, perhaps, Jung's affirmation of the validity of our subjective experience is critical for the involution that Teilhard deems necessary for evolution to reach its goal in Omega. Jung's study of Eastern yogas (spiritual practices and disciplines) gave him a glimpse into the reality that was largely missing from the West: interiority. This was the subject of his disagreement with Freud. Jung could not concede to an understanding of the psyche as driven by primal motives. He was aware of the power of consciousness and its transcendent capacities, and he sought to validate the many forms, levels, and expressions of consciousness through his work. Though Jung struggled to move beyond a gnostic understanding of the psyche, a testimony such as Teilhard's provides sound evidence that Jung's theories on the psyche were not only compelling but well-founded and legitimate.

Furthermore, Jung's methodology has opened the door for therapists looking for ways to integrate religion and spirituality into their practice. Teilhard's personal account of integration is an explicit description of his spiritual journey. We examined it, through a Jungian perspective, as a process of psychological growth and integration. However, it is possible to contemplate psychological development in the context of our spiritual evolution. We can explore our spiritual and psychological growth as complimentary processes leading us and the universe to greater wholeness of being.

6

The Synergy of Spirit and Psyche

THE DRIVE IN LIVING MATTER

Jung was open to the spiritual within his psychological theory. Yet, as a scientist, he refused to make any definitive statements about connections with his work and metaphysics. However, all sorts of psychotherapists emerged from Jung's initial school of thought. As these therapists came into their own, a variety of methods of Jungian psychoanalysis developed. Roberto Assagioli, an Italian psychiatrist and student of Jung's work, as well as his colleague, is credited with beginning a comprehensive psychoanalytic approach to human development known as *psychosynthesis*: a method of therapy that views our psychological development as a spiritual process.

Psychosynthesis is the "conscious attempt to *cooperate* with the natural process of growth—the tendency in each of us and in our world to harmonize and synthesize various aspects at ever higher levels of organization."[1] The emphasis on cooperation recognizes the existence of other real energies outside of strictly psychological ones.

Jung's approach limits the idea of God, or the Transcendent, to a purely psychological reality.[2] Though the psychological realm is as real as the physical, the gnostic view of God presents an existential barrier that becomes self-limiting as God is being defined by the ego, not the Self. Instead, psychosynthesis tries to recognize the "drive in living matter to perfect itself"[3] and then work *with* this thrust to achieve psychospiritual growth and transformation toward greater wholeness. Psychosynthesis demonstrates how real, higher psychospiritual energies are at work in the human person. It addresses the holistic journey that we must experience to achieve spiritual and psychological wholeness.

Psychosynthesis maintains that the human being must be viewed as a whole. While Eastern disciplines have tended to focus on the more esoteric dimensions of the psyche, Western practices have tinkered more with the personality and behavioral traits of the individual. Psychosynthesis recognizes both halves of the psyche in union. It demonstrates how an awareness of the whole (that is, the new third perspective, the Self) creates a vital connection with a transpersonal essence. Therapists John Firman and James Vargiu write, "In its broadest sense, psychosynthesis is a point of view and an attitude, from which to act with wisdom and love."[4] Psychosynthesis as a practice "holds that our opportunity in life is to manifest this essence, or Self, as fully as possible in the world of everyday personal and social existence."[5] In other words, if the core of the human psyche is in-tune with the innate drive to transcend, then the goal of psychosynthesis is to get the psyche in-tune with itself and this innate drive.

Assagioli's method focuses on higher aspects of the human personality. His approach to psychoanalysis is inclusive of the transcendent dimension of life. Assagioli's "egg model" of the psyche includes the conventional components of the psyche: the collective unconscious, our personal unconscious, our ego, and the Self, or what he calls *the Higher Self.*

Psychosynthesis recognizes an additional *superconscious* element of the psyche. The superconscious is "the realm from which originate our more highly evolved impulses: altruistic love and will, humanitarian action, artistic and scientific inspiration, philosophic and spiritual insight, and the drive for purpose and meaning."[6] The content of the superconscious often comes to us by way of dreams, visions, and religious or spiritual experiences. While Freud points out how repressing our biological drives can lead to suffering, Assagioli stresses that repression of the sublime can be equally as devastating. Denying any necessary aspect of our being—physical, mental, or spiritual—is catastrophic in our effort to grow in wholeness.

Throughout our lives, we get glimpses into the superconscious realm of our psyche. Our task is to integrate the content from the superconscious perspective, as it aids us in our psychological and spiritual growth. The focus of the superconscious is connecting our ego to the Higher Self. When we can integrate the content of the superconscious and enter into relationship with the Higher Self, we can "express the will of the Higher Self...achieved through wisdom and love—the two fundamental qualities of the consciousness of the Higher Self."[7] Assagioli describes the Higher Self as more than the archetype that represents our total psyche. The Higher Self is a conscious and embodied reality.

SYNTHESIZING THE SPIRITUAL AND PSYCHOLOGICAL

Psychosynthesis offers a psychological perspective that extends beyond traditional disciplinary orthodoxy and bridges into spirituality. In particular, psychosynthesis creates a point of connection between psychology and the spirituality of mystics like Teilhard. It acknowledges the transformation that occurs within our psyche as having a vital purpose within evolution. Just as the noosphere emerges from the biosphere, the Christosphere emerges from us as we grow personally and collectively. The human's *being* is transformed as it grows in self-awareness. Hence, it is no surprise for us to claim to feel "like a new person" after we have worked through a trying experience or grown in ways that take us beyond our presupposed limits.

The process of psychosynthesis helps to cooperatively facilitate the "drastic transmutation of 'normal' elements of the personality."[8] Once transpersonal integration begins, the personality begins functioning along a new interior dimension. Therefore, this inner transformation—as we observe time and time again with evolution's increase in complexity and consciousness—results in an external transformation. Our personality becomes integrated to recognize our place in a larger reality.

We find that we are connected to the universe through relationships, service, worship, work, and play. The act of full and conscious *being* is our connection to a cosmic history and a transcendent future. The discovery of our spiritual center and the conscious relationship we cultivate with our spiritual center are key in psychosynthesis.

Assagioli uses the term *spiritual* broadly, "always in reference to empirically observed human experience."[9] All of our experiences have spiritual value. Some possess values higher than others, whether it be of ethical, aesthetic, heroic, humanitarian, or altruistic origin. These experiences of higher values come from the higher conscious. The approach of psychosynthesis takes into consideration *all* the energies in the psyche and in the physical world. The Higher Self is the unifying center of these psychic (or spiritual) and physical energies.

Psychosynthesis operates in two primary stages: *personal psychosynthesis* and *transpersonal psychosynthesis*. First, in personal psychosynthesis, we develop an awareness of the *personal self* and integrate our personality. At this level of integration, we attain optimal functionality in our work and relationships by social standards.

Second, transpersonal psychosynthesis occurs when we learn how to integrate and express the energies of the *Transpersonal Self* (*Higher Self*). Through the Transpersonal Self, we "manifest such qualities as a broad sense of responsibility, a spirit of cooperation, altruistic love, a global perspective, and transpersonal purpose."[10] In personal synthesis we integrate the content of the lower unconscious, while in transpersonal synthesis we integrate the higher unconscious. One stage cannot occur without the other. Typically, there is overlap between the two stages. This creates a tension that can trigger a coincidence of opposites to be drawn into awareness, generating even more potential for integration. While we grow to become aware of our relation to transcendent realms, we must also "keep our feet on the ground" in the world to survive and contribute to the growth of evolution.

BREAKING DOWN BEFORE BREAKING THROUGH

Beyond the transpersonal experience and beyond psychosynthesis as a practice, there is the actual work of integration that occurs in the human being. There is the tangible evolution of our being. When we can endeavor through enough of our personal and transpersonal energies and achieve a level of balance and harmony within our psyche, a real transformation takes place. This can go the other way, as well, should we succumb to the pull of entropy, disintegration, and the "dark" forces of cosmic flux.

These dark forces are very real. Diminishment is necessary for the constant reconfiguration of energies that occurs in a dynamic cosmogenesis moving toward more advanced states of wholeness. It is only natural for things to break down so that they can become something new. A major theme in psychosynthesis is recognizing the crises, or "disturbances," that can occur when we begin to enter the process of psychosynthesis (voluntarily or involuntarily). These disturbances can be mental, emotional, and even physical where they take on symptoms of clinical conditions. However, Assagioli asserts that "in reality they have quite another meaning and function, and need to be dealt with in a very unique way."[11] Disturbances can range from ecstatic joy to overwhelming depression. They typically originate within conflicts between the "normal" drives and the conscious *I*, or between the individual and the outer world.

When our awareness begins to shift to the energies presenting themselves through the higher unconscious, our conscious state may become negligent of its own "lower" unconscious drives and tendencies. This can create a conflict between us and the world, which seems to overemphasize these lower drives. With an awareness of our "higher" drives alone, conflict can result "between some aspect of the personality and the progressive, emerging tendencies and aspirations of moral, religious, humanitarian, or spiritual character."[12] The nature of the disturbances can vary, and their duration is always limited. "After a while, it diminishes or ceases, and the flood is followed by the ebb. The personality was infused and transformed, but this transformation is seldom either permanent or complete."[13] We may exhibit symptoms identical to a neurosis or even psychosis, as our inner life begins to flood and overpower the ego's dominance. However, the disturbances initiated by higher drives result in a breakthrough of consciousness where it becomes reconstituted, or super-centered, upon the Higher Self.

SPIRITUAL AWAKENING

The breakdown that we experience before a birth into new consciousness is what Assagioli calls the *spiritual awakening*. "Awakening" is a symbolic expression that "suggests the becoming aware of a new area of experience, the opening of the hitherto closed eyes to an inner reality unknown."[14] The awakening is "spiritual" because it deals with the highly complexified inner life of the human person. Our highest qualities and values that raise our species up as a crowning achievement of cosmogenesis are what we can classify as "spiritual." Values such as "the ethical, the aesthetic, the heroic, the humanitarian and the altruistic"[15] define what it means to be human in our highest capacities. Such qualities are illustrative of a highly evolved consciousness.

In this way, the evolution of our psyche is as deliberate and intricate as the evolution of the universe. As the leading edge of evolution, *we* are the most current expression of life working to become more. Within this cosmic dynamism, psychosynthesis also stresses the steadfastness of the Transpersonal Self. Therefore, amid all the upheaval that can occur within psychic evolution, there is always the foothold for consciousness within the Center, or the Self. Though the Self may be the reason for upheaval at times, its function is intentional and purposeful in bringing our ego to the Center, where it can ultimately find integration in the balance of the Whole. Psychosynthesis holds that the Center, or Self, is *transpersonal*, because it is vitally different from the *personal self*, "the little self, or 'I,' usually identified with the ordinary personality, of which we are normally conscious."[16] It connects us with the transcendent.

When we can see our personal self in relationship with the Transpersonal Self, the vitality of this relationship allows us to experience the essential nature of our being. We awaken to ourselves as a unique and vital part of the cosmic whole. Assagioli defines these explicitly as "spiritual" experiences. Consciousness allows us to have spiritual experiences that reveal details about not simply our capacity for heightened states of awareness. We also learn there is a supreme value to this aspect of life. "Most spiritual experiences," says Assagioli, "contain a combination in various proportions of permanent changes, temporary changes, the cognition of obstacles that need to be overcome, and the lived realization of what it is like to exist at a higher level of integration."[17]

The higher level of awareness—call it Christ Consciousness, Buddha Awareness, Cosmic Consciousness, and so on—is not an end, but a means by which we can direct our attention toward meaning and purpose within a larger community and holistic worldview.[18] This consciousness "becomes an ideal model, a luminous beacon towards which one can navigate and which one can eventually achieve by his own means."[19] This is not to say that we are the masters of our own destiny, but we can become fantastic and devoted servants to a higher master, the Higher Self. When we view ourselves as a natural part of evolution, we get a better sense of real participation within "an organic process of inner growth and regeneration"[20] by allowing the changes to occur that the Higher Self calls us to experience. Expanded states of awareness cannot just be a head trip; they must be integrated and embodied. These experiences are often affirming and uplifting. Sometimes they can be "dark nights of the soul."

Assagioli acknowledges the reality of "the sufferings caused by periods of depression, by the ebbing and flowing of the inner life" as we journey through psychospiritual evolution. However, these low points "are abundantly compensated for by periods of renewed inflow of superconscious energies, and by the anticipation of the release and enhancement of the whole personality to be produced by Self-realization."[21] We participate more fully in reality through a more conscious and a more complex relationship with the Higher Self in which all is connected by growing in awareness of all the ways in which we are connected to the whole.

ATTRIBUTES OF PSYCHOSPIRITUAL TRANSFORMATION

Jesus, in the Gospel of Matthew, teaches, "Those who find their life will lose it, and those who lose their life for my sake will find it" (Matt 10:39). We are more than our bodies, more than our minds, more than our emotions, more than our education, more than our bank accounts, our jobs, or even our relationships.[22] We can feel vulnerable and small with the mindset that our being is limited to our physical body. Yet, through our steadfast immersion within the universe's commitment to driving through uncertainty and instability, we are able to find our way and we can flourish beyond this sense of smallness. It is these challenges that "make possible the breakthrough into spirit that is our birthright."[23] For when we converge with the Spirit, we are affirmed that we too are the Christ—composed of natures both human and divine—bound to and directed by the providence of cosmogenesis as creation moves to become what it is meant to be. Even the *Catechism of Catholic Church*, which Teilhard lived in tension with, reaffirms this notion of the human as the Christ: "Through the anointing of his Spirit who flows from the head to the members, [Christ] makes us other 'Christs'...God, indeed, who has predestined us to adoption as his sons, and conformed us to the glorious Body of Christ. So then you who have become sharers in Christ are appropriately called 'Christs.'"[24]

When it comes to describing the Higher Self or Christ Consciousness, only so much can be put into words. Legere says that "our words and even our images come up short" and that even "symbols...the language of the unconscious...do not adequately describe what we feel."[25] When we touch this almost ineffable state of being, we evolve *personally* into the final layer of evolution, the Christosphere. "The only thing that is the real coin of the realm—spiritually—is *experience*."[26] However, a survey of the people who have reached this level of consciousness provides clues as to what this state of being is like. Legere presents six qualities of a person who has experienced and lives from the vantage point of Christ Consciousness:[27]

1. *Unity*: A state of "radical interconnectedness" with all of creation has been the cornerstone of the writings of the experiences of mystics throughout history. In this state, there is a sense of "cosmic consciousness in which one feels a part of nature, connected to all creatures, at one with all that has ever existed, at one with all that will ever be." As the illusion of our separateness dissolves, we realize that "we represent one cell in a living organism called the Earth." Human beings are not the center of the operation. Instead, the internal, Christ Center is directing human efforts to the convergent unity that will reveal an emergent whole.
2. *Love*: Only a God, whose name is *love*, would be humbled, suffer, and die for humanity, so that the entire universe might experience atonement. Spiritual wayfarers who are integrated "sense a kinship with all creatures and a genuine appreciation for their value." The epitome of

love can be seen in Jesus, whose ministry was centered on love in the form of "opening up the heart to others." Opening the heart *to others* requires unconditional love. The ego tends to establish boundaries between the self and other, most commonly reducing "other" to an *object* upon which our self imposes itself as *subject*. In the state of Christ Consciousness, the boundaries of subject-object distinction are proved as illusion and the heart can express true compassion for the other. In Christ Consciousness, we "become aware of reality as a unified field of energy in which the material world, the individual, and the source of all phenomena, *Brahman* or the Absolute, are in essence identical with each other."[28]

3. *Joy*: When we embody a spiritually evolved consciousness, joy becomes our disposition. We do not take ourselves or the "small stuff" in life too seriously. We live in the manner where, according to St. Julian of Norwich, "all is well and all manner of things will be well." This ineffable joy allows us to "live big...free from a stingy or restricted manner." Joy is not conditional upon sensual stimulation as is pleasure. It may be felt as pleasure by the body, but joy is the result of tapping into something even deeper—true Spirit.
4. *Peace*: In one way or another, spiritually evolved people have a sense of inner peace. They have journeyed within and found a seasoned calmness that comes from learning to withstand and work with the torrents of the psyche as it grows. More importantly, we realize that the only order of business upon returning to the "normal" world is to have faith and live in a way that encourages and empowers radical unity among all. We acknowledge our mission regardless of the struggles it might entail. We are at peace because we realize that

our earthly mission is larger than ourselves. Doing so allows us to detach from the results, even if this means the extreme of facing the end of our life on earth.

5. *Service*: The quality of service embodied by the Higher Self is very similar to love. If we truly have evolved spiritually, then we have experienced the selfless love of God and know nothing but to reflect that divine love through our being. As Teilhard says, "To communicate itself, my ego must subsist through abandoning itself or the gift will fade away."[29] This is how we access our human genetic hardware at its core. In-tune with our Higher Self, we exist in a dimension where spirit is *primary* and allows us to encounter God's unconditional love in all things. By virtue of our physical being-in-the-world, we must emanate a love reflective of that of the love found at the Center. This is basic Teilhardian philosophy; moreover, it is a law of the universe. If consciousness increases, it must express itself in some way, shape, or form. Service becomes an outpouring of the inner Higher Self into the external realm. Embracing our spiritual insights makes us more practical and more beneficial to the world.
6. *Creativity*: "When one has, to some extent, literally seen the light and felt the power and experienced the love, the individual often reports feeling like a co-creator with the Divine." When we encounter and embody the Higher Self, we access the highest level of wholeness in evolution's Omega. Our being is composed of the very atoms that make up the presumably infinite number of stars in the universe. Humanity reflects this radical diversity through its creativity. "The creativity may express itself in writing, in organizing a soup kitchen, painting, sculpture, in organizing a protest march or

> a petition drive...the possibilities are endless." This quality perhaps epitomizes the proper placement of our ego, or "me" consciousness, because an authentically creative person shows a greater willingness to take chances and make mistakes—we no longer have the drive to survive, but to flourish. We recognize the feeling of being a "channel" for something greater that inspires and directs our creativity.

Teilhard poetically describes how we embody Divine creativity:

> I merge myself through my heart with the very heart of God. God is at the tip of my pen, my spade, my brush, my needle; of my heart and of my thought. By pressing the stroke, the line or the stitch on which I am engaged, I shall lay hold of that last end towards which my inmost self tends.[30]

As we grow psychospiritually, evolution makes a quantum leap with us. The world grows to be a fuller manifestation of the wholeness that we experience within. Inevitably, human evolution is tied up with cosmic evolution. From the transpersonal perspective of Teilhard and all of time's great mystics, we become aware that every small action and grain of thought has a direct influence on our personal growth and on the larger evolution of the universe.

7

How to Live in the Divine Milieu

THE HUMAN PERSON, THE DIVINE, AND COSMIC WHOLENESS

When Teilhard answered the call to serve in the French army during World War I, he chose to be a stretcher bearer. This role put him on the front line of the conflict. Being on "the front" was important for Teilhard. He understood the front of the war to also be the front of evolution's advance toward greater being. Whatever humanity was trying to achieve through this monumental effort and voluntary immersion into violence and chaos, Teilhard wanted to be a part of it. The front demanded an immediacy of presence, focus, and unwavering devotion to accomplishing his mission.

We are also called to "the front" of evolution. Unlike Teilhard and the many other brave souls who have experienced the chaos of combat, we do not need to be engaged in kinetic conflict to get a sense of the front. Rather, we must be willing to consciously take up the task of allowing the front of evolution to unfold within us. We are called to do the difficult work of individuating and integrating this cosmic endeavor into a personal sense of wholeness and fullness. We must be present to our experiences while remaining focused on the small tasks that help to complete our larger mission. It is easy to get ahead of ourselves or to live in the past. The front calls us to live in present tension of what it means to be human, to discover our authentic Self, and to live in a way that is personally connected to the universe. The front demands our total commitment to working toward a goal that is beyond us—a transpersonal goal.

Assagioli's model diagrams how our psyche integrates content from "lower" levels to "higher" levels. Teilhard's model of evolution shows how elements aggregate from simple to more complex levels of connection, moving from a lower degree of consciousness to a higher level. Teilhard offers the idea that when humanity becomes super-centered, collectively united in Christ Omega, we are *transformed*. Consciousness is no longer the same as it once was. Nor is humanity and nor is life as we know it. The transformed consciousness is definitive of a new kind of life, *super-life*.

Super-life can be understood in three ways:

First, the biological understanding explains how life triumphs over death on the level of competing elements. Structures may break down, but the elements that make up the structures can be reformed in novel ways.

Second, on a religious level, super-life is the triumph of life over death through humanity encountering Divinity in a most final way. This can be referred to as *immortality*, a concept encapsulated in words like *salvation* and *atonement*.

Third, super-life can be understood as the "access of the person to the collective conscious life that, by transcending individual conscious life, prepares the higher life engendered by the union of personal centers and persons in a hyperpersonal focal point of love and irreversibility."[1] Super-life is the point where evolution becomes totally self-aware through our human experience of self-awareness, both as an individual and as a collective organism.

Super-life is essentially a "threshold of reflection"[2] where an ultra-synthesis occurs as individual human units form a collective whole, a human organism, which is centered upon the Omega Point. Teilhard sees the advent of super-life occurring with increasing intensity "probably over hundreds of centuries yet to come."[3] Super-life is the result of the process of super-personalization. Super-personalization is when, "in the final analysis, sympathy and unanimity (since the forces of love alone possess the property of personalizing by unifying),"[4] are expressed by humanity and thus reveal the emergent face of Christ Omega. Super-life is when life, as we currently know it on earth, is transformed in a way that the whole of creation comes into union with the Divine in Christ.

SUPRA-PERSONALIZATION

Teilhard also uses the prefix *supra-* to describe our collective transformation. Only when we go *beyond* ourselves to unite does our fullest Self emerge. Teilhard writes, "Union made us human by organizing, under the control of a thinking spirit, the confused powers of matter. It will now make us 'super-human' by making us into elements subject to some higher soul. Internal union has personalized us so far. Now external union is going to 'supra-personalize' us."[5]

The tendency for elements to be drawn into creative union to reveal the emergence of more complex and more conscious structures unfolds within our life as individuals and as a human collective. Living in these seemingly chaotic times, it might seem like Teilhard's vision of union in Omega is a pipedream. He acknowledges the possibility of humanity totally falling apart into disintegration along with the earth. Yet this idea runs counter to the ascent of evolution toward more complexity and more consciousness. If we phrase our situation as living through a time of *awakening*, it better captures the whole of our experience and does not deny the abundance of grace present in the world for those with the eyes to see.

The supra-personal is our collective awareness of the whole. "The whole," in this case, means not only the whole human organism, but also the entire universe. When crossing the threshold from the personal to the supra-personal, cosmogenesis becomes *Christogenesis*. There is a shift from a centered and then decentered consciousness to a super-centered consciousness. Christogenesis occurs because of cosmogenesis. Supra-personalization organically unites the Christian faith with cosmic evolution. The heart of our belief emerges as the heart of the universe.

In one sense, "Christian faith" can be seen as the confessional, dogmatic faith of Christianity. On a more inclusive level, "Christian faith" can be understood as the consciousness with which we center ourselves to unite with the larger whole in a participatory way that is, at its highest form, personally transformative. Jesus never commanded us to worship him. Jesus only asked that we follow him.

For Teilhard, Christogenesis, described by St. Paul as the *Pleroma*, is the ultimate expression of our human evolution. The Pleroma can be understood as the Mystical Body or the Total Christ. In the Pleroma, we, through the human organism, are organically unified with the Mystical Body of Christ, as seen in the theology of St. Paul, as well. The emergence of Christ Consciousness in Christogenesis is "nothing other than an extension of noogenesis in which cosmogenesis culminates,"[6] or the next stage of evolution.

THE DIVINE MILIEU

As Teilhard's spiritual vision matured, he found it was possible for God to be found in our everyday lives. Lou Savary writes how, from Teilhard's perspective, "everything we learn about creation is something we are learning about the Body of Christ—the Christ that lives today, the Christ who is as big as the cosmos."[7] As a result, Teilhard cultivated a radically new kind of spirituality. Teilhard's spirituality holds together God, the world, and humanity's conscious role in relationship. He recorded his unique approach to spirituality in a collection of personal and spiritual reflections entitled *The Divine Milieu*.

Savary explains Teilhard's goal in *The Divine Milieu* as "finding a way to classify all the events of our lives to see how they all fit into the divine milieu and the love of the Cosmic Christ."[8] The divine milieu is a layer of reality (in the same way that the noosphere is a layer of reality) that the human person can become aware of. We can only become aware of this reality through encountering the Personal; that is, we must encounter the Divine in a way that is most intimate and relatable to us.

The easiest analogy for understanding the presence of the divine milieu in which Teilhard says we live is, perhaps, like a fish in water. The fish needs the water to survive and will die without it, yet the fish is not aware of the water unless it is removed from the water. In the same way, it becomes so easy for us to remain unaware of God's ever-present and self-offering nature.

It is true that many people typically do not become aware of their dependence on God or some understanding of a higher power, until they have exhausted all other options of self-reliance and have hit some kind of "rock bottom." However, it is also true that many people have undergone instruction that has presented them with a God confined to cathedrals and catechisms, reserved for access only in the high heavens, and not actively and dynamically present in the whole of creation (God of the Above). Teilhard received a formation that was both of the Church and of the world. His experiences formed him in a way where his understanding of his faith stood up to the test of the crucible of the world and his empirical knowledge of its evolutionary laws.

In *The Divine Milieu,* Teilhard seeks "to teach how to see God everywhere, to see him in all that is most hidden, most solid, and most ultimate in the world...bringing it to true form and perfection."[9] Teilhard demonstrates how, through true loving intention, human *activities*—what we do by our own effort—can become divinized. We can give back to God through the outpouring of our self in service of the world. This emptying of ourselves, or *kenosis,* becomes fertile ground in which we live anew in Christ through *theosis,* or sharing in divinity.

Teilhard also shows how our *passivities*—what we must endure—can be divinized. Activities and passivities are deeply entwined. For example, if a student is taking certain prerequisite courses to earn a specific degree, the student's *activity* of taking a required class is actually a passivity, because the student must take the class to attain the degree. Yet the student's engagement with the class, its professor, the material, and his or her classmates become the activities through which the experience can be transformed.

Teilhard helps us see how classifying activities and passivities is dependent on our perspective. He acknowledges that passivities, because they stretch so far beyond our conscious actions and thoughts, are "immeasurably the wider and the deeper part."[10] We can, however, act consciously in response to the passivities we undergo. We can sanctify our passivities and our activities.

Through the sanctification of our activities and passivities, the product of our interactions forms the mystical union between humanity and God. As we bless our lives and the world, our awareness of our sacred relationship to all of creation grows in abundance. "In fact, for Teilhard, the mystical union of the members or cells of Christ's Body is a system far richer and more real than any biological system or human social system."[11] Our system's functionality is influenced by our intentions combined with our activities. It is also greatly impacted by how well we endure the suffering and pain often connected with our passivities. Yet, the system is ultimately dependent on Christ. Therefore, even when we turn away from the Transcendent and step outside of participation in the bigger picture, the divine milieu continues to exist. It continues to allure us to share in its resonance. It is vibrant in the lives of those who pulse with the love that is continually offered through Christ's relationship to the creation. It beckons all for the benefit and fullness of all. Our real and embodied expression of Divine love is the emergence of Omega, the second coming of Christ in the fullness of the Pleroma as Christ Consciousness.

TRANS-MATTER SPIRITUALITY

The emergence of our Christ Consciousness is a spiritual transformation, or a spiritualization of matter. Matter makes beings "capable of unification" and it is matter "through which the multitudinous monads are bound together."[12] Matter makes the expression of higher forms of consciousness (Spirit) possible. In *The Divine Milieu*, Teilhard writes, "By matter we are nourished, lifted up, linked to everything else, invaded by life."[13] Matter is to be blessed and acclaimed. Thomas King reflects on his own interaction with matter:

> My spirit partially animates and partially effects the matter of the entire universe, and the spirits of all other people partially animate and effect the same matter. Because of matter all things are partially in my control and partially

> escape my control. Through my matter I am vulnerable; through my matter I do not have the autonomy I might desire. But matter is also that which enables me to escape myself and enter into a wider world—or is it into nothingness?[14]

King goes on to recognize the numinous character of matter that evokes both "fear and fascination" as he feels himself drawn to the deepest levels of matter where, like Teilhard, he states, "perhaps in faith I believe this is where I will meet my God, for He has descended into the lowest parts of the Earth." As a result, King declares,

> Matter becomes my way of salvation....Like the bread that is eaten and loses its form as bread in order to be transformed into the one who has consumed it, so must I descend into a somewhat formless matter in order to be transformed into the Christ who has also descended there in order to rise, filling all things....This is the "trans-matter" spirituality of Teilhard.[15]

Teilhard's *trans-matter spirituality* allows him to be in union with God through the world. A trans-matter spirituality maintains the tension between the opposite poles of the universal and the Personal. Within a trans-matter spirituality, these polarities are united in the Cosmic Christ. The two halves of this term—"Cosmic" and "Christ"—maintain the tension between the terms of evolution in the cosmic sense and in the Christic sense, our sense of our humanity and our sense to become *more*. The transcendent third appears when we live in the conscious tension of our humanity spiraling in ascent to reveal our divinity.

The human person, writes King, is "the gateway through which the rising all is reaching for God."[16] When we embrace the notion of God within ourselves, we, through the Cosmic Christ, begin partaking in a spirituality that is more integrated with the world. Our spirituality is not separated into distinct spheres—but as a total sphere, a *Christosphere*, in which the Personal, encountered as the total sphere, is expressive of the uniquely differentiated spheres that bring all into union.

A trans-matter spirituality may supplement traditional practices that we use to connect to the divine. It goes beyond orthodoxy to include *the whole universe* through which all meets the All. A synthesis emerges and we can say "that [we] love God with [our] whole body and soul, and with the *whole universe*."[17] We are no longer an unconscious fragment of reality, detached from the whole. We are transformed as a conscious and divinized part of the whole. We are an "in-gathering of the Earth brought to consciousness."[18] Therefore, when we say that we love God, it is not through belief in doctrine and dogma that this love is expressed. Rather, it is through the very act of *being* and our contribution to the larger whole. Teilhard noticed how the human must love the Divine "with every fiber of the unifying universe."[19] In return, "as through a sacred door...God passes through [the human] into all things."[20] The more we allow ourselves to pass into God through our relationship with the world, the more we allow God to pass into us.

Therefore, just as there is a Cosmic Omega, there is also a personal point in the conscious human journey where we assume a new identity to live for God, as in the example of Paul changing his name from Saul. We might consider this a "little Omega Point" within the larger, total Omega. When we can evolve to this point, a real transformation happens allowing us access to a new state of being. We become aware of the reality of our inner, psychospiritual landscape, as well as the transcendent horizon that evolution pulls us toward. Most importantly, we become aware of how to join meaningfully within this delicate performance.

THE ULTRA-PHYSICS OF THE INTERIOR LIFE

The Divine Milieu outlines a spiritual dynamic suitable for today's interconnected and rapidly evolving world. Teilhard offers that an entirely new discipline relating our subjective experience in an objective sense can help "measure" our discernment as we seek fullness in God. He calls this discipline "ultra-physics" or "hyper physics."

Teilhard uses the science of ultra-physics to replace metaphysics by encompassing what is happening *without* to what is happening *within* elements as they work to unite in creative union. In Teilhard's words, ultra-physics is the discipline "in which matter and spirit would be englobed in one and the same coherent and homogeneous explanation of the world."[21]

Ultra-physics begins as a phenomenological variable from "physico-chemical matter and leads across the discontinuous thresholds of life and spirit to phenomenological meaning and, finally, ontological and spiritual sense."[22] Teilhard sees ultra-physics as a guide to reaching higher forms of personality, becoming essential as evolution begins supra-personalizing:

> I should be happy to see you...substituting for a metaphysics that is stifling us an ultra-physics in which matter and spirit would be englobed in one and the same coherent and homogenous explanation of the world.... Thought will explode or evaporate unless the universe, in response to humanization, becomes divinized in some way....Christianity is the only living phylum that retains a divine personality.[23]

In a world where the sharing of genes has been rivaled by the sharing of ideas and data, Teilhard sees the new discipline of ultra-physics as crucial in evolution's ascent to wholeness. The goal of ultra-physics is to help us bridge the falsely perceived separation between spirit and matter. Ultra-physics is when consciousness has "developed beyond the present stage of noosphereic consciousness through co-reflection unanimized and elevated by planetization, thus already centered on Omega."[24] Ultra-physics is best seen through ultra-humans, or spiritually and psychologically integrated people. The ultra-human possesses the actualization of the capacity for *ultra-reflectivity*, or *ultra-reflection*—the sense of how to seek and find the Divine.

The simplest way to understand ultra-physics is to follow Teilhard's lead of having faith in the world and loving God. With ultra-physics, we integrate our understanding of the world with our inner yearning for wholeness. We can mature in how we perceive and interact with the world and people outside us, and we can mature in how we interact with the inner world of spirit and psyche. We can grow and mature in *relationship*. The fuller this sense of relationship in our lives, the more likely it is that we are applying and living what Teilhard calls ultra-physics. We take all that we are, and in offering up in service to the Omega Point, we are blessed, and we bless all we are in relationship with.

Living in what is currently considered to be a "post-truth age," we can use Teilhard's ultra-physics to help us navigate disorder and chaos as we attempt to discern what is true. We can be open to conflicting stories and perspectives, holding them in tension without the need to make rash judgments or decisions. We can sift through the data while remaining grounded in principle questions such as:

How does this move us toward the Omega Point?

How does this increase conscious relationship within the world?

How does this encourage union *and* preserve the identity of the individual person?

LIVING WHOLLY IN THE DIVINE MILIEU

The *Divine Milieu* empowers us in a way that validates our journey to a life of fullness and wholeness. According to Teilhard, "At the peak of their adherence to [God], the elect also discovers in him the consummation of their individual fulfillment." This is not accomplished through a mysticism that dissolves our sense of self in order to become one with the universe and God. Rather, Teilhard writes that Christianity grasps "the essential aspiration of all mysticism: *to be united* (that is, to become one with the other) *while remaining oneself*."[25]

Ultimately, the *milieu* molds humanity for what is revealed in St. Paul and St. John:

> It is the quantitative repletion and the qualitative consummation of all things: it is the mysterious Pleroma, in which the substantial *one* and the created *many* fuse without confusion in a *whole* which, without adding anything essential to God, will nevertheless be a sort of triumph and generalization of being.[26]

The repletion and consummation of all things that occurs in the Pleroma—the totality of wholeness—also reveals a larger communion in which the human plays a vital role. Teilhard writes,

> From the beginning of the Messianic preparation, up till the Parousia, passing through the historic Jesus and the phases of growth of his Church, a single event has been developing in the world: the Incarnation, realized in each individual, through the Eucharist.
>
> All the communions of a life-time are one communion.
>
> All the communions of all [humans] now living are one communion.

> All the communions of all [humans], present, past and future, are one communion.[27]

This sense of communion is what allows us to reach out beyond our individual sense of being and into a network of more conscious inter-being. Teilhard sees this network as bound together by charity. He writes, "Christian charity, which is preached about so fervently in the Gospels, is nothing else than the more or less conscious cohesion of souls engendered by their communal convergence *in Christo Jesu*." This is because "it is impossible to love Christ without loving others… and it is impossible to love others (in a spirit of broad human communion) without moving towards Christ."[28] Teilhard describes how the "individual divine *milieux*, in proportion as they establish themselves, tend to fuse with one another."[29] He writes "that the only human embrace capable of worthily enfolding the divine is that of all [humans] opening their arms to call down and welcome the Fire." Teilhard's conclusion is clear: "The only subject ultimately capable of mystical transfiguration is the whole group of [hu]mankind forming a single body and a single soul in charity."[30] The unity of consciousness is created as individuals are drawn toward "the other" in a way that is "not by simple personal sympathy, but by what is much higher: *the united affinities of a world for itself, and of that world for God*."[31]

Teilhard rejected "mysticisms that neither accepted responsibility for the ongoing creation nor made full use of the power of the human to love and to act."[32] Teilhard was troubled that people would often look to mysticism as an escape from the world, rather than be injected even deeper into its midst. For if we are seeking union with the All, then we must grab hold of evolution's natural ascent, remaining steadfast through its troubles and travails, as we climb toward wholeness in its pinnacle.

Fortunately, his approach "provides a solid motivation for work that is in harmony with the goals of the Cosmic Christ."[33]

Teilhard was not satisfied with dualistic thinking, "balancing the rational and the numinous, the reasonable and the aesthetic, the scientific and the spiritual," as he "waited patiently for his subjective world and objective world to reveal a single truth,"[34] when he faced paradoxes, especially those involving faith and science. Maintaining the tension between perceived opposites resulted in the emergence of "a common substratum of aspirations and illuminations"[35] and allowed access to a third and transcendent perspective. The Cosmic Christ—human, divine, and cosmic—is Teilhard's testament to this tension and its value in our lives.

This transcendent perspective, or Transcendent Function, reveals a greater dimension of our own self. Teilhard came to recognize his Higher Self was one with the Cosmic Christ. This allowed him to trust his vision that evolution was completed and united in the warmth of Christ's love. Duffy writes that "whenever his inner experience, his desires, and his dreams coincided with the direction of nature's evolutionary path, he trusted his insight and experienced what he called a complete act of knowing."[36] Thomas King affirms this insight: "In the very act of scientifically knowing, [Teilhard] knew God."[37] Teilhard came to know God through the awareness that his very being was part of the universe and was moving with evolution in the ascent to wholeness in God.

Conclusion

KNOW THYSELF

In essence, Teilhard came to know God through knowing himself. He began by tracing his cosmic lineage deep into the heart of matter, and then he committed himself to the ascent of evolution, working to build the future. He achieved a sense of wholeness through relationship with God by encountering the Divine in all things. Yet, it was through his own person that he felt closest to God.

Teilhard teaches us that the Divine Presence fills, animates, unifies, and expresses its personal character through the universe, but most immediately and intimately through our very being. He affirms that our joys, accomplishments, challenges, suffering, and hopes are all part of a larger network of being. Most importantly, Teilhard's work ethic shows how critical it is that we integrate our experiences into our lives.

His thought demonstrates how his own work evolved from his initial inklings of God's presence in creation to the spiritual power of matter to transform life through forces of chaos, order, diminishment, and growth. He took diligent notes as a paleontologist looking for archaic remnants within the world, and he recorded his findings from his inner world with equal zeal. In order to take those notes, he was completely present in his observations. We must also be present to be able to train our mystic vision—or as Teilhard calls it, our ability to *see*.

Additionally, it is helpful for us to keep some documentation of our personal growth, especially our spiritual growth. What we call a "spiritual experience" can often be fleeting and ephemeral. It is critical that we record it in some way. Recording it allows us to hold on a bit longer, perhaps more as an observer, yet with a memento of a moment that moved us. We might keep a journal, draw, dance, play music, converse with a trusted friend, or meet with a spiritual director or counselor. We might embed the event within an oral tradition, create a ritual, or preserve its memory as an anniversary. These practices allow us to revisit the event in a way to reawaken our insights and integrate them in a more holistic sense. We learn how to be more aware of God in all things.

Teilhard had a proclivity for writing his ideas repeatedly as his vision evolved and matured. From his early writings before the First World War, through his final journal entry a few days before his death in New York City, Teilhard consistently documented his experiences and his thoughts. As Teilhard grew as a person and experienced the world, he found that his vision of God became clearer. He wrote his personal credo on two occasions, first in 1934, then in 1950. Teilhard's credo reflects his personal story:

> I believe the universe is an evolution;
> I believe evolution proceeds towards spirit;
> I believe spirit, in human beings, completes itself in the personal;
> I believe the supreme personal is the Universal Christ.[1]

In his personal story, Teilhard tells of a scattered perception of the Divine in the first circle, simply a Presence. As he continues through his circles, his vision of God becomes clearer; and his synthesis complete in the Personal. In the same way, his credo begins with identifying the current of evolution moving toward spirit. Spirit is complete when the human person comes into relationship with the supreme personal, the Universal Christ. Teilhard's psychospiritual integration is ultimately expressed through his emphasis on *seeing* or in some way being aware of our relationship to a larger whole. This is necessary to feel a sense of personal wholeness.

THE SPIRITUAL POWER OF MATTER

The sense of wholeness that Teilhard writes about has been expressed by mystics throughout the ages. Yet, Teilhard's vision is so unique because it brings focus to the spiritual power of matter. By nature of our presence in the world, we participate in a dynamic universe that is unfolding.

We must remember that evolution can be chaotic by nature, and we must consciously enter into this chaos to discern its purpose and direction in our larger growth and in the bigger picture of the universe. Teilhard, Jung, and Assagioli encountered chaos in their lives. Each man responded by engaging the apparent disorder to discover the implicit yet unseen order. They longed for the *why* of their epoch, seeking not just meaning and reason for why things were in such a condition: They were more focused on the goal or end-state of the process and where it was taking humanity.

Teilhard's vision focuses on the evolution of consciousness from the planetary perspective. The Omega Point becomes an emergent reality when humanity unites in consciousness. Although Jung recognized that consciousness had been evolving over time, he paid particular attention to the growth of the consciousness within the individual human person. Assagioli brings these two perspectives together by synthesizing the growth of the human psyche as a spiritual process. Teilhard saw evolution as a process of spiritualization and personalization. Thus, psychosynthesis clarifies how our spiritual needs are as vital as our biological and social needs. Furthermore, Assagioli's mapping of "higher" dimensions of the psyche is useful for illustrating how consciousness evolves to a more integrated awareness of oneself, the world, and the Divine. As evolution reaches new levels of psychic development, it also achieves greater spiritual development wherein there is a clearer expression of the authentic human, the ultra-human.

The vision of all three thinkers overlaps with the Transcendent as the necessary component for completion and wholeness. In Teilhard's thought, the Omega Point is three parts evolution and one part transcendent God. Jung's method highlights how three-becomes-four wherein the integration of the contents of the unconscious (the inferior function) reveals the Self, or the Transcendent Function. Though Assagioli recognizes the importance of the collective unconscious, personal unconscious, and ego, he directs the practice of psychosynthesis toward the higher unconscious, wherein by integrating our spiritual and transcendent experiences, we become a fuller embodiment of the Transpersonal Self. Both cases mirror Teilhard's existential dialectic where we move from centration, to decentration, to super-centration in our quest for happiness, fullness, and wholeness in our lives.

Teilhard's documentation of his psychospiritual growth is invaluable because he provides a practical pathway where we can learn to *see* and encounter wholeness within our own person. Wholeness is not found in our person, alone, but through our relationship to the All *within us*. The God who creates the universe created us who exist in the universe. God can and should be encountered in the world and in others, yet we must first discover the God who lives in us to be able to relate to the world in the fullest depth and breadth possible for us personally. God becomes known with greater clarity through an increase and evolution in the levels of depth, relationality, and wholeness in our life. Growth toward authentic and healthy personal fulfillment is growth toward God. Our personal growth toward completion in the Personal is a vital development within the total organism of humanity.

LOVE SO GREAT IT MOVES THE SUN AND OTHER STARS

Know oneself, and know God. Teilhard writes, "No, you do not ask anything false or unattainable of me. You merely, through your revelation and your grace, force what is most human in me to become conscious of itself at least."[2] Certainly, the things that are "most human" in our lives are often not appealing at first. However, when seen with the proper perspective, these incredibly humbling qualities that we possess might be seen as elements of our being that are in a state of becoming in our journey to become whole and live a life rich in happiness and fulfillment.

Though traveling the road to wholeness is hardly ever easy, there is consolation in knowing that we walk this road together. Though our lives may be self-contradictory at times, it is through our struggles that we adapt to unify and become expressive of a higher center within us and within the world. War, racism, and injustice on a global scale make it difficult to embrace this perspective. However, Teilhard's urging is to go deeper, to find a value in suffering and chaos, and to charge action full of meaning so that humanity might "venture forth, resting upon [Christ], into the uncharted ocean of charity."[3] While Teilhard had the advantage of possessing a scientific understanding of the world, he is not the first person to touch a greater reality by pursuing a higher calling. His multifaceted perspective is what allows his thought to be helpful to so many. Teilhard's work is rich in imagery of the natural world and thus offers a planetary perspective for contemplating the Divine.

Like the many cells that function in harmony to maintain homeostasis in the larger organism they form, we can become conscious of our relationship to the universal pulse, the incendiary heartbeat at the center of the cosmos. We can dive into the heart of matter of our own beings and from there we can find other beings with whom we resonate.

The elements of the universe are allured by the love of Omega, the love that the poet Dante describes as *L'amor che move il sole e l'altre stelle*, the love so great that it moves the sun and other stars. In the *Divine Milieu*, the Personal and Universal are revealed in union in the Cosmic Christ. Through the gift of self-reflection, we must access this cosmic love that radiates from our core. Accessing this love allows us to become whole and to share in even greater wholeness through uniting with others. Teilhard writes, "The greater man becomes, the more humanity becomes united, with consciousness of, and master of, its potentialities, the more beautiful creation will be, the more perfect adoration will become, and the more Christ will find, for mystical extensions, a body worthy of resurrection."[4]

Teilhard teaches us that there is value found by entering the heart of things, especially when it involves facing challenge, struggle, and chaos in an evolving world. These are necessary tensions in the growth of the planet and of consciousness. The challenge now is not the struggle to develop more powerful processors, more destructive weapons, or more self-organizing and intelligent machines. Our task now is to love more consciously and with the entire complexity of our being, more than we have loved before. As we do the inner work necessary to love more wholly, we contribute to the sacred synergy of spirit and psyche, evolving with the universe to wholeness in the Omega Point.

Notes

CHAPTER 1

1. Kenneth Sørensen and Hanne Birkholm, "Roberto Assagioli—His Life and Work, a Biography," trans. Gunnar Hansen, website of Kenneth Sørensen, May 2, 2017, https://kennethsorensen.dk/en/roberto-assagioli-his-life-and-work/, accessed February 4, 2024.

2. Carl Jung, *Psychology and Alchemy,* vol. 12 of *The Collected Works of C. G. Jung*, 2nd ed. (Routledge, 1980), par. 152.

3. Pierre Teilhard de Chardin, *The Future of Man*, trans. Norman Denny (Harper and Row, 1964), 67.

4. Pierre Teilhard de Chardin, *The Heart of Matter*, trans. René Hague (Harcourt Brace Jovanovich, 1978), 74.

5. John A. Sanford, *Mystical Christianity: A Psychological Commentary on the Gospel of John* (Crossroad, 2000), 215.

6. Pierre Teilhard de Chardin, *Hymn of the Universe*, trans. Simon Bartholomew (Harper and Row, 1961), 21.

7. Pierre Teilhard de Chardin, *The Divine Milieu* (Harper and Row, 1960), 70.

8. Pierre Teilhard de Chardin, *The Making of a Mind: Letters from a Soldier-Priest [1914–1919]* (Harper & Row, 1965), 306.

9. Pierre Teilhard de Chardin, *The Future of Man*, trans. Norman Denny (Harper and Row, 1964), 67.

10. Teilhard de Chardin, *Future of Man*, 67.

11. Teilhard de Chardin, *Future of Man*, 67.

12. Teilhard de Chardin, *The Making of a Mind*, 58.

13. Pierre Teilhard de Chardin, *Towards the Future* (Harcourt Brace Jovanovich, 1975), 117.

14. Teilhard de Chardin, *Towards the Future*, 77.

15. Teilhard de Chardin, *The Heart of Matter*, 129.

16. Teilhard de Chardin, *The Future of Man*, 55–56.

17. Teilhard de Chardin, *The Future of Man*, 55–56.

18. Ronald Modras, *Ignatian Humanism: A Dynamic Spirituality for the 21st Century* (Loyola Press, 2004), 46.

19. Teilhard de Chardin, *The Divine Milieu*, 126.

20. Kathleen Duffy, *Teilhard's Mysticism: Seeing the Inner Face of Evolution* (Orbis Books, 2014), 46.

21. Pierre Teilhard de Chardin, *The Phenomenon of Man*, trans. Bernard Wall (Harper and Row, 1959), 56–57.

22. Pierre Teilhard de Chardin, *Letters to Leontine Zanta, 1923–39* (Harper and Row, 1969), 87.

23. Pierre Teilhard de Chardin, *The Appearance of Man* (Harper and Row, 1969), 139.

24. Pierre Teilhard de Chardin, *Christianity and Evolution*, trans René Hague (Harcourt Brace Jovanovich, 1969), 107–8.

25. Teilhard de Chardin, *The Phenomenon of Man*, 56, 60.

26. Pierre Teilhard de Chardin, *Writings in Time of War*, trans. René Hague (Harper and Row, 1968), 137.

27. Teilhard de Chardin, *Christianity and Evolution*, 106.

28. Duffy, *Teilhard's Mysticism*, 89.

CHAPTER 2

1. Pierre Teilhard de Chardin, *The Phenomenon of Man*, trans. Bernard Wall (Harper and Row, 1959), 29.

2. Thomas M. King, *Jung's Four and Some Philosophers: A Paradigm for Philosophy* (Notre Dame Press, 1999), 276.

3. Pierre Teilhard de Chardin, *Human Energy*, trans. J. M. Cohen (Harcourt Brace Jovanovich, 1969), 145.

4. Teilhard de Chardin, *The Phenomenon of Man*, 268–72.

5. Kathleen Duffy, *Teilhard's Mysticism: Seeing the Inner Face of Evolution* (Orbis Books, 2014), 64.

6. Pierre Teilhard de Chardin, *The Heart of Matter*, trans. René Hague (Harcourt Brace Jovanovich, 1978), 94.

7. Teilhard de Chardin, *Heart of Matter*, 94.

8. Teilhard de Chardin, *Heart of Matter*, 94.

9. Teilhard de Chardin, *Heart of Matter*, 96.

10. Teilhard de Chardin, *Activation of Energy: Enlightening Reflections on Spiritual Energy*, trans. René Hague (Harcourt, Inc., 1976), 313.

11. Teilhard de Chardin, *The Heart of Matter*, 100.

12. Teilhard de Chardin, *The Heart of Matter*, 16.

13. Teilhard de Chardin, *The Heart of Matter*, 96.

14. Pierre Teilhard de Chardin, *Christianity and Evolution*, trans. René Hague (Harcourt Brace Jovanovich, 1969), 8.

15. Teilhard de Chardin, *The Phenomenon of Man*, 327.

16. Teilhard de Chardin, *The Phenomenon of Man*, 293–94.

17. Thomas E. Legere, *Living an Authentic Life* (AuthorHouse, 2007), 198.

18. Christopher Mooney, "The Body of Christ in the Writings of Teilhard de Chardin," *Theological Studies* 25 (1964): 586.

19. Teilhard de Chardin, *Towards the Future* (Harcourt Brace Jovanovich, 1975), 198–99.

20. Pierre Teilhard de Chardin, *Letters from a Traveler* (Harper and Row, 1962), 245.

21. Teilhard de Chardin, *The Heart of Matter*, 40.

22. Sion Cowell, *The Teilhard Lexicon: Understanding the Language, Terminology, and Vision of the Writings of Pierre*

Teilhard de Chardin (Liverpool University Press, 2004), 179.

23. Teilhard de Chardin, *Human Energy*, 96.

24. Hippolytus, *Elucidations*, ed. James Donaldson and Alexander Roberts (Edinburgh, 1867), 30.

25. Hippolytus, *Elucidations*, 30.

26. Ursula King, *Teilhard de Chardin and Eastern Religions: Spirituality and Mysticism in an Evolutionary World* (Paulist Press, 2011), 42.

27. Teilhard de Chardin, *Christianity and Evolution*, 58.

28. Teilhard de Chardin, *The Phenomenon of Man*, 31.

CHAPTER 3

1. Pierre Teilhard de Chardin, *The Heart of Matter*, trans. René Hague (Harcourt Brace Jovanovich, 1978), 50.

2. Thomas M. King, *Teilhard's Mass: Approaches to "The Mass on the World"* (Paulist Press, 2005), vii.

3. King, *Teilhard's Mass*, vii.

4. "The Mystical Milieu" is found in Pierre Teilhard de Chardin, *Writings in Time of War*, trans. René Hague (Harper and Row, 1968).

5. Mary Lukas and Ellen Lukas, *Teilhard* (Doubleday, 1977), 339.

6. Pierre Teilhard de Chardin, *Letters from a Traveler* (Harper and Row, 1962), 66.

7. Pierre Teilhard de Chardin, *The Divine Milieu* (Harper and Row, 1960), 129.

8. Teilhard de Chardin, *Writings in Time of War*, 246.

9. Teilhard de Chardin, *The Divine Milieu*, 130.

10. Pierre Teilhard de Chardin, *Letters to Two Friends 1926–1952*, trans. Helen Weaver, ed. Ruth Nanda Anshen (New American Library, 1967), 123.

11. Kathleen Duffy, *Teilhard's Mysticism: Seeing the Inner Face of Evolution* (Orbis Books, 2014), 27.

12. Claude Cuénot, *Teilhard de Chardin: A Biographical Study*, trans. V. Colimore (Burns and Oates, 1965), 190.
13. Cuénot, *Teilhard de Chardin*, 91.
14. Pierre Teilhard de Chardin, *Hymn of the Universe*, trans. Simon Bartholomew (Harper and Row, 1961), 44.
15. Teilhard de Chardin, *Writings in Time of War*, 119.
16. Teilhard de Chardin, *The Divine Milieu*, 130.
17. Teilhard de Chardin, *Letters to Two Friends*, 44.
18. Teilhard de Chardin, *Letters to Two Friends*, 31.
19. Pierre Teilhard de Chardin, *Science and Christ*, trans. René Hague (Harper and Row, 1968), 39.
20. Teilhard de Chardin, *The Divine Milieu*, 120.
21. Duffy, *Teilhard's Mysticism*, 30.
22. Teilhard de Chardin, *The Heart of Matter*, 20.
23. Teilhard de Chardin, *Writings in Time of War*, 123.
24. Joel Primack and Nancy Abrams, *View from the Center of the Universe: Discovering Our Extraordinary Place in the Cosmos* (Riverhead Books, 2006), 99.
25. Primack and Abrams, *View from the Center of the Universe*, 99.
26. Duffy, *Teilhard's Mysticism*, 43.
27. Duffy, *Teilhard's Mysticism*, 53.
28. Teilhard de Chardin, *Writings in Time of War*, 124.
29. Teilhard de Chardin, *Writings in Time of War*, 124.
30. Ilia Delio, "Evolution and the Rise of the Secular God," in *From Teilhard to Omega: Co-Creating an Unfinished Universe*, ed. Ilia Delio (Orbis Books, 2014), 41.
31. Duffy, *Teilhard's Mysticism*, 56.
32. Duffy, *Teilhard's Mysticism*, 60.
33. Teilhard de Chardin, *The Divine Milieu*, 70.
34. Duffy, *Teilhard's Mysticism*, 75.
35. Teilhard de Chardin, *Writings in Time of War*, 124.
36. Teilhard de Chardin, *Writings in Time of War*, 71.
37. Duffy, *Teilhard's Mysticism*, 77.

38. Teilhard de Chardin, *The Heart of Matter*, 204.
39. Teilhard de Chardin, *The Divine Milieu*, 76–77.
40. King, *Teilhard's Mass*, 80.
41. Teilhard de Chardin, *The Divine Milieu*, 77.
42. Teilhard de Chardin, *Christianity and Evolution*, 16.
43. Teilhard de Chardin, *The Divine Milieu*, 143.
44. Teilhard de Chardin, *The Divine Milieu*, 76–77.
45. Duffy, *Teilhard's Mysticism*, 84.
46. King, *Teilhard's Mass*, 60–61.
47. Teilhard de Chardin, *Science and Christ*, 89.
48. Pierre Teilhard de Chardin, *The Phenomenon of Man*, trans. Bernard Wall (Harper and Row, 1959), 38.
49. Teilhard de Chardin, *Christianity and Evolution*, 106.
50. Teilhard de Chardin, *The Phenomenon of Man*, 4.
51. Teilhard de Chardin, *The Vision of the Past*, trans. René Hague (Harper and Row, 1968), 73.
52. Teilhard de Chardin, *The Phenomenon of Man*, 95.
53. Teilhard de Chardin, *The Phenomenon of Man*, 142.
54. Teilhard de Chardin, *Human Energy*, trans. J. M. Cohen (Harcourt Brace Jovanovich, 1969), 136.
55. Duffy, *Teilhard's Mysticism*, 90.
56. Teilhard de Chardin, *Writings in Time of War*, 137.
57. Teilhard de Chardin, *Science and Christ*, 45.
58. Duffy, *Teilhard's Mysticism*, 89.
59. Duffy, *Teilhard's Mysticism*, 99.
60. Teilhard de Chardin, *The Divine Milieu*, 79.
61. Duffy, *Teilhard's Mysticism*, 114.
62. Duffy, *Teilhard's Mysticism*, 112.
63. Teilhard de Chardin, *Writings in Time of War*, 131.
64. Teilhard de Chardin, *The Heart of Matter*, 212.
65. Ursula King, *Spirit of Fire: The Life and Vision of Teilhard de Chardin* (Orbis Books, 1996), 22–23.
66. Duffy, *Teilhard's Mysticism*, 110.
67. Duffy, *Teilhard's Mysticism*, 113.

68. Teilhard de Chardin, *The Heart of Matter*, 82–83.
69. Duffy, *Teilhard's Mysticism*, 112.
70. Teilhard de Chardin, *The Heart of Matter*, 124.
71. Teilhard de Chardin, *The Heart of Matter*, 175–76.
72. Omega, the final letter of the Greek alphabet, is a reference to the fullness of Christ at the end of time as established by Christ in Revelation (Rev 22:13).
73. Teilhard de Chardin, *Christianity and Evolution*, 116.
74. Teilhard de Chardin, *The Heart of Matter*, 121.
75. King, *Teilhard's Mass*, 113.
76. Teilhard de Chardin, *The Heart of Matter*, 74.
77. King, *Teilhard's Mass*, 117.
78. Teilhard de Chardin, *The Heart of Matter*, 130.
79. Teilhard de Chardin, *The Heart of Matter*, 130.
80. Teilhard de Chardin, *Science and Christ*, 136.
81. Teilhard de Chardin, *Science and Christ*, 85.

CHAPTER 4

1. W. E. Cooper, "William James's Theory of the Self," *The Monist* 75, no. 4 (1992): 504.
2. David Hothersall, *History of Psychology*, 4th ed. (McGraw-Hill, 2004), 290.
3. Robert A. Johnson, *Inner Work: Using Dreams and Active Imagination for Inner Growth* (HarperCollins, 1986), 6.
4. Johnson, *Inner Work*, 6.
5. Anthony Stevens, *Jung: A Brief Insight* (Sterling, 2011), 190.
6. Johnson, *Inner Work*, 6.
7. Johnson, *Inner Work*, 11.
8. Johnson, *Inner Work*, 11.
9. Pierre Teilhard de Chardin, *Science and Christ*, trans. René Hague (Harper and Row, 1968), 45.
10. Johnson, *Inner Work*, 11.

11. Thomas M. King, *Jung's Four and Some Philosophers: A Paradigm for Philosophy* (Notre Dame Press, 1999), 292.

12. King, *Jung's Four*, 292.

13. King, *Jung's Four*, 292.

14. Pierre Teilhard de Chardin, *The Phenomenon of Man*, trans. Bernard Wall (Harper and Row, 1959), 186.

15. Kathleen Duffy, *Teilhard's Mysticism: Seeing the Inner Face of Evolution* (Orbis Books, 2014), 60.

16. Johnson, *Inner Work*, 6.

17. Johnson, *Inner Work*, 7.

18. Ram Dass, "The Ego: A Dichotomy of Fear and Love," Listening Heart Series, last modified August 11, 2015, accessed January 22, 2024, https://www.ramdass.org/the-ego-dichotomy-fear-love/.

19. Thomas E. Legere, *Living an Authentic Life* (AuthorHouse, 2007), 15.

20. Legere, *Living an Authentic Life*, 15.

21. Legere, *Living an Authentic Life*, 15.

22. Legere, *Living an Authentic Life*, 17–18.

23. Legere, *Living an Authentic Life*, 25.

24. Carl Jung, *Two Essays on Analytical Psychology*, vol. 7 of *The Collected Works of C.G. Jung* (Princeton University Press, 1967), 305.

25. Jeffrey Miller, *The Transcendent Function: Jung's Model for Psychological Growth Through Dialogue with the Unconscious* (SUNY Press, 2004), 99.

26. Miller, *The Transcendent Function*, 100.

27. Steven Pinker, *How the Mind Works* (W.W. Norton, 1997), 234.

28. Julian Jaynes, *The Origins of Consciousness in the Breakdown of the Bicameral Mind* (Houghton-Mifflin, 1976), 100–125.

29. Miller, *The Transcendent Function*, 30.

30. Miller, *The Transcendent Function*, 3.

31. Miller, *The Transcendent Function*, 3.

32. Miller, *The Transcendent Function*, 6.

33. Miller, *The Transcendent Function*, 102.

34. Marie-Louise Von Franz, "The Process of Individuation," in *Man and His Symbols*, eds. Carl Jung and Marie-Louise Von Franz (Doubleday, 1964), 211.

35. Von Franz, "The Process of Individuation," 211.

36. Carl Jung, *The Structure and Dynamics of the Psyche*, vol. 8 of *The Collected Works of C.G. Jung* (Princeton University Press, 1970), 798.

37. Jung, *The Structure and Dynamics of the Psyche*, 342.

38. Jung, *The Structure and Dynamics of the Psyche*, 325.

39. Carl Jung, *Aion: Researches into the Phenomenology of the Self*, vol. 9, part 2 of *Collected Work of C.G. Jung*, 2nd ed. (Routledge, 1991), par. 70.

40. Carl Jung, *Psychology and Religion: West and East*, vol. 11 of *The Collected Works of C.G. Jung* (Routledge, 1991), par. 226–30.

41. Jung, *Psychology and Religion*, par. 226–30.

42. Jung, *Psychology and Religion*, par. 226–30.

43. Jung, *Psychology and Religion*, par. 233.

CHAPTER 5

1. Thomas M. King, *Jung's Four and Some Philosophers: A Paradigm for Philosophy* (Notre Dame Press, 1999), 17.

2. John A. Sanford, *The Kingdom Within: The Inner Meaning of Jesus' Sayings* (Harper Collins Publishers, 1987), 20.

3. Sanford, *The Kingdom Within*, 20–21.

4. Sanford, *The Kingdom Within*, 20–21.

5. Pierre Teilhard de Chardin, *Letters from a Traveler* (Harper and Row, 1962), 50.

6. Teilhard de Chardin, *Letters from a Traveler*, 50.

7. Thomas King, *Jung's Four*, 268–69.

8. Pierre Teilhard de Chardin, *Writings in Time of War*, trans. René Hague (Harper and Row, 1968), 25. The brackets with the French *sentir* are an addition by Thomas King in *Jung's Four*.

9. King, *Jung's Four*, 269.

10. Teilhard de Chardin, *Writings in Time of War*, 25.

11. Teilhard de Chardin, *Writings in Time of War*, 25.

12. King, *Jung's Four*, 269.

13. King, *Jung's Four*, 269.

14. Teilhard de Chardin, *Writings in Time of War*, 25.

15. Teilhard de Chardin, *Writings in Time of War*, 27.

16. Teilhard de Chardin, *Writings in Time of War*, 32.

17. King, *Jung's Four*, 270.

18. Teilhard de Chardin, *Writings in Time of War*, 32.

19. Teilhard de Chardin, *Writings in Time of War*, 32.

20. King, *Jung's Four*, 271.

21. King, *Jung's Four*, 271.

22. King, *Jung's Four*, 273.

23. Teilhard de Chardin, *Writings in Time of War*, 32.

24. Teilhard de Chardin, *Writings in Time of War*, 125.

25. King, *Jung's Four*, 272.

26. Teilhard de Chardin, *Writings in Time of War*, 127.

27. Teilhard de Chardin, *Writings in Time of War*, 127.

28. Teilhard de Chardin, *Writings in Time of War*, 59.

29. King, *Jung's Four*, 274–75.

30. Teilhard de Chardin, *Writings in Time of War*, 120.

31. Teilhard de Chardin, *Writings in Time of War*, 122.

32. Teilhard de Chardin, *Writings in Time of War*, 146.

33. Pierre Teilhard de Chardin, *The Heart of Matter*, trans. René Hague (Harcourt Brace Jovanovich, 1978), 175–76.

34. King, *Jung's Four*, 274.

35. Teilhard de Chardin, *Writings in Time of War*, 187.

36. King, *Jung's Four*, 275.

37. King, *Jung's Four*, 288.

38. King, *Jung's Four*, 288.

39. Teilhard de Chardin, *The Phenomenon of Man*, 259.
40. King, *Jung's Four*, 288.
41. Teilhard de Chardin, *The Phenomenon of Man*, 170.
42. Teilhard de Chardin, *The Phenomenon of Man*, 307, 309.

CHAPTER 6

1. John Firman and James Vargiu, "What Is Psychosynthesis?," *Synthesis* 3–4 (1974): 144.
2. Robert A. Johnson, *We: Understanding The Psychology of Romantic Love* (HarperCollins, 1983), 64.
3. Firman and Vargiu, "What Is Psychosynthesis?," 144.
4. Firman and Vargiu, "What Is Psychosynthesis?," 144.
5. Firman and Vargiu, "What Is Psychosynthesis?," 144.
6. Firman and Vargiu, "What Is Psychosynthesis?," 144.
7. Firman and Vargiu, "What Is Psychosynthesis?," 147.
8. Firman and Vargiu, "What Is Psychosynthesis?," 147.
9. Roberto Assagioli, "Self-Realization and Psychological Disturbances," *Synthesis* 3–4 (1974): 148.
10. Firman and Vargiu, "What Is Psychosynthesis?," 147.
11. Assagioli, "Self-Realization and Psychological Disturbances," 149.
12. Assagioli, "Self-Realization and Psychological Disturbances," 149.
13. Assagioli, "Self-Realization and Psychological Disturbances," 157.
14. Assagioli, "Self-Realization and Psychological Disturbances," 150.
15. Assagioli, "Self-Realization and Psychological Disturbances," 149.
16. Assagioli, "Self-Realization and Psychological Disturbances," 156.
17. Assagioli, "Self-Realization and Psychological Disturbances," 159.

18. These terms all embody or are at least analogs to what Teilhard refers to in the "ultra-human" or one who has "christic consciousness."

19. Assagioli, "Self-Realization and Psychological Disturbances," 159.

20. Assagioli, "Self-Realization and Psychological Disturbances," 170.

21. Assagioli, "Self-Realization and Psychological Disturbances," 170.

22. Thomas E. Legere, *Living an Authentic Life* (AuthorHouse, 2007), 133.

23. Legere, *Living an Authentic Life*, 133.

24. *Catechism of the Catholic Church* (USCC Publication Services, 1993), Article 733.

25. Legere, *Living an Authentic Life*, 194.

26. Legere, *Living an Authentic Life*, 194.

27. Legere, *Living an Authentic Life*, 196–205.

28. Ken Wilber, *The Spectrum of Consciousness*, 2nd ed. (Quest Books, 1993), 84.

29. Pierre Teilhard de Chardin, *The Phenomenon of Man*, trans. Bernard Wall (Harper and Row, 1959), 251.

30. Pierre Teilhard de Chardin, *Divine Milieu* (Harper and Row, 1960), 64.

CHAPTER 7

1. Siôn Cowell, *The Teilhard Lexicon: Understanding the Language, Terminology, and Vision of the Writings of Pierre Teilhard de Chardin* (Sussex Academic Press, 2001), 184.

2. Cowell, *The Teilhard Lexicon*, 184.

3. Pierre Teilhard de Chardin, *Letters from a Traveler* (Harper and Row, 1962), 450.

4. Pierre Teilhard de Chardin, *Science and Christ*, trans. René Hague (Harper and Row, 1968), 160.

5. Pierre Teilhard de Chardin, *Human Energy*, trans. J. M. Cohen (Harcourt Brace Jovanovich, 1969), 63.
6. Teilhard de Chardin, *Human Energy*, 63.
7. Louis M. Savary, *Teilhard de Chardin: The Divine Milieu Explained; A Spirituality for the 21st Century* (Paulist Press, 2007), xiii.
8. Savary, *Divine Milieu Explained*, 39.
9. Pierre Teilhard de Chardin, *The Divine Milieu* (Harper and Row, 1960), 9–10.
10. Teilhard de Chardin, *The Divine Milieu,* 12.
11. Savary, *The Divine Milieu Explained*, 66.
12. Pierre Teilhard de Chardin, *Hymn of the Universe*, trans. Simon Bartholomew (Harper and Row, 1961), 69.
13. Teilhard de Chardin, *The Divine Milieu*, 106.
14. Thomas M. King, *Teilhard's Mysticism of Knowing* (Seabury Press, 1981), 69.
15. King, *Teilhard's Mysticism of Knowing*, 69–70.
16. King, *Teilhard's Mysticism of Knowing*, 82.
17. Pierre Teilhard de Chardin, *Human Energy*, 159; *Science and Christ*, 172; *The Heart of Matter,* 101.
18. Pierre Teilhard de Chardin, *The Phenomenon of Man*, trans. Bernard Wall (Harper and Row, 1959), 297.
19. Teilhard de Chardin, *The Phenomenon of Man*, 297.
20. Pierre Teilhard de Chardin, *Writings in Time of War,* trans. René Hague (Harper and Row, 1968), 144.
21. Pierre Teilhard de Chardin, *Accomplir l'homme: Lettres inédites (1926–1952)*, letter to Christophe Gaudefroy, October 11, 1936 (Grasset, 1968), 110.
22. Cowell, *Teilhard Lexicon*, 203.
23. Teilhard de Chardin, *Accomplir l'homme*, 110, 111–12.
24. Cowell, *The Teilhard Lexicon*, 203.
25. Teilhard de Chardin, *The Divine Milieu*, 88.
26. Teilhard de Chardin, *The Divine Milieu*, 95.
27. Teilhard de Chardin, *The Divine Milieu*, 96–97.

28. Teilhard de Chardin, *The Divine Milieu*, 120.
29. Teilhard de Chardin, *The Divine Milieu*, 120.
30. Teilhard de Chardin, *The Divine Milieu*, 121.
31. Teilhard de Chardin, *The Divine Milieu*, 122.
32. Duffy, *Teilhard's Mysticism*, 121.
33. Duffy, *Teilhard's Mysticism*, 121.
34. Duffy, *Teilhard's Mysticism*, 124.
35. Teilhard de Chardin, *Christianity and Evolution*, 97.
36. Duffy, *Teilhard's Mysticism*, 124.
37. King, *Teilhard's Mysticism of Knowing*, vii.

CONCLUSION

1. Pierre Teilhard de Chardin, *How I Believe* (Harper and Row, 1934), 96; *The Heart of Matter* (Harcourt Brace & Company, 1950), 78.
2. Pierre Teilhard de Chardin, *The Divine Milieu* (Harper and Row, 1960), 123.
3. Teilhard de Chardin, *The Divine Milieu*, 123.
4. Teilhard de Chardin, *The Divine Milieu*, 133.

Bibliography

Assagioli, Roberto. "Self-Realization and Psychological Disturbances." *Synthesis*, nos. 3–4 (1974): 148–71.

Catechism of the Catholic Church. USCC Publication Services, 1993.

Cooper, W. E. "William James's Theory of the Self." *The Monist* 75, no. 4 (1992): 504–20.

Cowell, Siôn. *The Teilhard Lexicon: Understanding the Language, Terminology, and Vision of the Writings of Pierre Teilhard de Chardin*. Sussex Academic Press, 2001.

Cuénot, Claude. *Teilhard de Chardin: A Biographical Study*. Translated by V. Colimore. Burns and Oates, 1965.

Dass, Ram. "The Ego: A Dichotomy of Fear and Love." Listening Heart Series. Ram Dass. Last modified August 11, 2015. Accessed November 22, 2017. https://www.ramdass.org/the-ego-dichotomy-fear-love/.

Delio, Ilia. "Evolution and the Rise of the Secular God." In *From Teilhard to Omega: Co-Creating an Unfinished Universe*, edited by Ilia Delio. Orbis Books, 2014.

Duffy, Kathleen. *Teilhard's Mysticism: Seeing the Inner Face of Evolution*. Orbis Books, 2014.

Firman, John, and James Vargiu. "What Is Psychosynthesis?" *Synthesis*, nos. 3–4 (1974): 144–47.

Haldane, J. B. S. *Possible Worlds, and Other Papers*. Harper & Bros., 1928.

Hippolytus. *Elucidations*. Edited by James Donaldson and Alexander Roberts. T&T Clark, 1867.

Hothersall, David. *History of Psychology*. 4th ed. McGraw-Hill, 2004.

Jaynes, Julian. *The Origins of Consciousness in the Breakdown of the Bicameral Mind*. Houghton-Mifflin, 1976.

Johnson, Robert A. *Inner Work: Using Dreams and Active Imagination for Inner Growth*. HarperCollins, 1986.

———. *We: Understanding the Psychology of Romantic Love*. HarperCollins, 1983.

Jung, Carl G. *Aion: Researches into the Phenomenology of the Self*. Vol. 9, part 2 of *The Collected Works of C.G. Jung*. 2nd ed. Routledge, 1991.

———. *The Archetypes and the Collective Unconscious*. Vol. 9, part 1 of *The Collected Works of C. G. Jung*. 2nd ed. Translated by R. F. C. Hull. Princeton, NJ: Princeton University Press, 1981.

———. *Contributions to Analytical Psychology*. Harcourt Brace, 1928.

———. *Man and His Symbols*. Edited by Carl Jung and Marie-Louise Von Franz. Doubleday, 1964.

———. *Psychology and Alchemy*. Vol. 12 of *The Collected Works of C. G. Jung*. 2nd ed. London: Routledge, 1980.

———. *Psychology and Religion: West and East*. Vol. 11 of *The Collected Works of C. G. Jung*. Princeton University Press, 1970.

———. *The Structure and Dynamics of the Psyche*. Vol 8 of *The Collected Works of C. G. Jung*. Princeton University Press, 1970.

———. *Two Essays on Analytical Psychology*. Vol. 7 of *The Collected Works of C. G. Jung*. Princeton University Press, 1967.

King, Thomas M. *Jung's Four and Some Philosophers: A Paradigm for Philosophy*. Notre Dame Press, 1999.

———. *Teilhard's Mass: Approaches to "The Mass on the World."* Paulist Press, 2005.

———. *Teilhard's Mysticism of Knowing.* New York: Seabury Press, 1981.

King, Ursula. *Spirit of Fire: The Life and Vision of Teilhard de Chardin*. Orbis Books, 1996.

———. *Teilhard de Chardin and Eastern Religions: Spirituality and Mysticism in an Evolutionary World*. Paulist Press, 2011.

Legere, Thomas E. *Living an Authentic Life*. AuthorHouse, 2007.

Lukas, Mary, and Ellen Lukas. *Teilhard*. Doubleday, 1977.

Miller, Jeffrey. *The Transcendent Function: Jung's Model for Psychological Growth Through Dialogue with the Unconscious*. SUNY Press, 2004.

Modras, Ronald. *Ignatian Humanism: A Dynamic Spirituality for the 21st Century*. Loyola Press, 2004.

Mooney, Christopher. "The Body of Christ in the Writings of Teilhard de Chardin." *Theological Studies* (December 1964): 576–610.

Panikkar, Raimon. *The Rhythm of Being: The Gifford Lectures*. Orbis Books, 2010.

Pinker, Steven. *How the Mind Works*. W.W. Norton, 1997.

Primack, Joel, and Nancy Abrams. *View from the Center of the Universe: Discovering Our Extraordinary Place in the Cosmos*. Riverhead Books, 2006.

Sanford, John A. *The Kingdom Within: The Inner Meaning of Jesus' Sayings*. HarperCollins Publishers, 1987.

———. *Mystical Christianity: A Psychological Commentary on the Gospel of John.* Crossroad, 2000.

Savary, Louis M. *Teilhard de Chardin: The Divine Milieu Explained: A Spirituality for the 21st Century.* Paulist Press, 2007.

Soelle, Dorothee. *The Silent Cry: Mysticism and Resistance*. Fortress Press, 2001.

Sørensen, Kenneth, and Hanne Birkholm. "Roberto Assagioli—His Life and Work." Translated by Gunnar Hansen. Website of Kenneth Sørensen, May 2, 2017. https://kennethsorensen.dk/en/roberto-assagioli-his-life-and-work/. Accessed February 4, 2024.

Stevens, Anthony. *Jung: A Brief Insight*. Sterling, 2011.

Teilhard de Chardin, Pierre. *Accomplir l'homme: Lettres inédites (1926–1952)*. Grasset, 1968.

———. *Activation of Energy*. Harcourt Brace Jovanovich, 1970.

———. *The Appearance of Man*. Harper and Row, 1965.

———. *Christianity and Evolution*. Translated by René Hague. Harcourt Brace Jovanovich, 1969.

———. *The Divine Milieu*. Harper and Row, 1960.

———. *The Future of Man*. Translated by Norman Denny. Harper and Row, 1964.

———. *The Heart of Matter*. Translated by René Hague. Harcourt Brace Jovanovich, 1978.

———. *Human Energy*. Translated by J. M. Cohen. Harcourt Brace Jovanovich, 1969.

———. *Hymn of the Universe*. Translated by Simon Bartholomew. Harper and Row, 1961.

———. *Letters from a Traveler*. Harper and Row, 1962.

———. *Letters to Leontine Zanta, 1923–39*. Harper and Row, 1969.

———. *Letters to Two Friends, 1926–1952*. Translated by Helen Weaver. Edited by Ruth Nanda Anshen. New American Library, 1967.

———. *The Phenomenon of Man*. Translated by Bernard Wall. Harper and Row, 1959.

———. *Science and Christ*. Translated by René Hague. Harper and Row, 1968.

———. *Toward the Future*. Harcourt Brace Jovanovich, 1975.

———. *The Vision of the Past*. Translated by René Hague. Harper and Row, 1968.

———. *Writings in Time of War*. Translated by René Hague. Harper and Row, 1968.

Von Franz, Marie-Louise. "The Process of Individuation." In *Man and His Symbols*, edited by Carl Jung and Marie-Louise Von Franz. Doubleday, 1964.

Wilber, Ken. *The Spectrum of Consciousness*. 2nd ed. Quest Books, 1993.